P9-DMO-678

MORE TALES OF A LOW-RENT BIRDER

More Tales of a Low-Rent Birder

by Pete Dunne

DRAWINGS BY KEITH HANSEN

FOREWORD BY KENN KAUFMAN

ABA-ND
6.16.94
To: Burt —
Kindred Spirit

University of Texas Press, Austin

Printed in the United States of America
First edition, 1994

♾ The paper used in this publication meets the
minimum requirements of American National Standard
for Information Sciences—Permanence of Paper
for Printed Library Materials, ANSI Z39.48-1984.

LIBRARY OF CONGRESS
CATALOGING-IN-PUBLICATION DATA

Dunne, Pete, date
More tales of a low-rent birder / by Pete Dunne ; drawings by Keith Hansen ; foreword by Kenn Kaufman. — 1st ed.
p. cm.
ISBN 0-292-71572-2 (cloth)
1. Bird watching—North America. 2. Birds—North America.
I. Title.
QL681.D88 1994
598'.072347—dc20 93-47657

Earlier versions of these essays appeared
in *American Birds, Birder's World, Living Bird Quarterly,*
and the New Jersey Sunday Section of the *New York Times.*

This book is dedicated to
FLOYD P. WOLFARTH,
friend and mentor, whose opinions
were invariably shared by God-in-Heaven
(even if Floyd was occasionally too modest
to point this out himself).

Contents

More Tales of a Low-Rent Birder

Foreword

BY KENN KAUFMAN

Imagine yourself as a stranger, a newcomer, walking into a huge room where the birders of North America have gathered. The room is filled with activity and conversation. Clusters of experts are debating minor details; bird-listers are comparing their lists; birders of every stripe are trading stories. You pause at the door, uncertain, but then a young man walks up to greet you. "Hi!" he says. "Come on in. Join the fun. Let me show you around." Quick impressions . . . scuffed tennis shoes, faded jeans, cheap T-shirt, good binoculars. Firm handshake, warm and engaging smile. No need to ask: this is Pete Dunne.

The only thing wrong with this picture is that you could never get all the birders to gather in one room. A room large enough has never been built, and those birders are too independent and diverse. Since about 1970 there has been a tremendous growth in the popularity of bird watching on this continent. At the same time, an explosion of information has multiplied the amount of bird knowledge available. Expert birders today are likely to know far more than the experts of three decades ago. So as the birding community has grown, the gulf between what the beginner knows and what the expert knows has also grown wider and wider.

That's one of the reasons why Pete Dunne's writings are so valuable. Pete is undeniably a top birder, but he writes most of his material for people who are not. And he writes a lot. He cranks out articles, columns, and essays for a remarkable variety of publications. Any newcomer to birding, metaphorically walking into that big room, probably would be met at the door by one of Pete's essays—and welcomed. In Dunne's birding world, shared interest is the only coin of the realm, and even the rank novice is respected. Scorn is reserved for the know-it-all birder who would somehow discourage a beginner.

From my viewpoint, it seems the only sad birder is the one who knows it all, who has seen everything. I hate going out in the field with people like that. Give me the enthusiasm of a beginner who goes crazy on seeing a cardinal for the first time. Sure, the cardinal *is* a dirt-common bird, but it's a beautiful one; and the wise birder should go crazy over the thousandth cardinal as well as the first. But we sometimes lose sight of this. When we're discussing the timing of molt of the tertials on *Empidonax* flycatchers, or something equally arcane, we may momentarily lose our ability to get excited about the robins and chickadees in the back yard.

So if we need an intermediary, an ambassador to the person-on-the-street, we'll send Pete Dunne. And why not? After all, Pete can masquerade as an ordinary guy for minutes at a time. He grew up in the suburbs. He likes dogs, likes sports cars, likes sports. The girl he married, Linda Ellis, is pretty enough to be his (or anyone's) high school sweetheart. Out with a bunch of teenagers, Dunne proves that he can handle a Frisbee or a baseball as easily as a spotting scope. In person as well as in print, he often comes across as a sort of All-American boy birder, Huckleberry Finn with a pair of the latest 10 × 40s.

It would be hard to analyze the character of Huck Finn without discussing the Mississippi River, and it's similarly hard to talk about Pete Dunne without at least mentioning New Jersey. Pete has been a Jerseyite all his life. Many a hotshot birder would have viewed this as a handicap. As recently as the mid-1970s, none of us would have listed New Jersey as a prime birding destination; it had a couple of good spots, but otherwise we viewed it as industrialized, populated, the back lot between Philadelphia and New York. Many of us, had we awakened to find ourselves living in New Jersey, would have started packing immediately to move elsewhere. Dunne's way was different: he stayed, and promoted New Jersey birding.

And he did so with remarkable effect. The autumn hawk flight down at Cape May had been known for decades, in a general way. But Dunne's systematic counts (and enthusiastic write-ups) in the late 1970s turned it into a major birding event, with hundreds of watchers coming from far and wide to see the hawks go by. An even bigger coup was Dunne's idea of a "World Series of Birding" to be held every May in New Jersey. It was crazy, but it caught on, and it has been getting bigger every year. Birders flock to New Jersey every May, and the news media take notice. When a team from Ontario won the tenth-anniversary competition, in 1993, it made headlines all across Canada.

So, spring and fall, people are coming from all over North America (and elsewhere) for the great fun of birding in New Jersey. Nowadays it seems only natural that so many of Dunne's essays should focus on this prime birding state.

The setting for the stories, therefore, is often the same. The topic always pertains to some aspect of nature or birding. But the approach boxes the compass, because Pete finds an astonishing variety of different angles on his subject matter. Science fiction, allegories, ghost stories, hyperbole, outrageous lies, any approach is fair game so long as it gets some point across.

In fact, disgruntled copyeditors may sometimes feel that Pete is having just a little too much fun. But that's only half the story. When I invoked the spirit of Huck Finn I was not thinking of any sappy Disney version, but of something closer to Mark Twain's original character. The original Finn had levels of deeper meaning beneath that aw-shucks exterior. Ditto for Dunne. All his birding-is-fun writing has to be done in his spare time, because forty hours a week, Pete is working for the New Jersey Audubon Society—struggling to save some habitat for the birds in that increasingly developed state. This is the other side of the coin. It gives his essays their bite. Beneath the freewheeling surface runs a set of deeper themes: birds, and other aspects of wild nature, are important both scientifically and spiritually; nature is faced with increasing threats in today's world; we should all appreciate nature and help to save it. This undercurrent is always there in Dunne's writing. Even when it does not break the surface, it adds strength and significance to every essay, including those in the collection you are holding now.

If all the birders had gathered in one room (probably somewhere in New Jersey), the guy painting wonderful wild bird murals all over the walls would be a Californian named Keith Hansen. I first met this artist in 1976, the same year that Dunne was to do the first full-season hawk count at Cape May. Although we were only kids, with no money, Keith and I promptly took off for a madcap attempt to see all the birds of Mexico in five big weeks. Keith was already an artist of wild originality, drawing mystical trogons, aquatic parrots, phantasmagorical toucans and hummingbirds that never existed. In the time since, his technique has matured—but fortunately, his imagination has not. Keith Hansen's bird art is like no one else's. He can work the same kind of wizardry with images that Pete Dunne can with words, which is saying a lot. Getting these two masters in the same book is a magical feat indeed.

In closing, I have to say that I have one serious complaint about Pete's writing. Not about the quality—nothing wrong with that. At his best, Dunne is one of the finest nature writers ever. No one else can describe the birders and their pursuits with so much insight, imagination, and gentle humor.

No, my complaint is that Pete's essays appear in too many different places, so it's hard for his fans to catch them all. We were all very pleased a few years ago when he brought out an initial greatest-hits volume with the whimsical title *Tales of a Low-Rent Birder.* The thousands of readers who loved that book will be excited to know that the writer is back—thanks to the University of Texas Press—with a collection of *More Tales* in the same genre. And even if you've somehow missed Pete's writing in the past, I advise you to heed our opening invitation: Come on in. Join the fun. Let Pete Dunne and Keith Hansen show you around. I think you'll soon agree that if you go with the right guides, the Low-Rent district offers some of the best birding anywhere.

Preface

I am sometimes asked whether I consider myself to be a birder who is a writer or a writer who goes birding. The truth is I don't distinguish. The act of birding and the expression of those experiences seem irrevocably bound to me. This book, then, is a culling of twenty-five essays, the synthesis of many thousands of experiences that have been lived and penned. All focus upon some aspect of birds, birders, or birding. All require just one thing to bring them to life in your hands—the catalytic touch of your own personal experiences in the field.

Unlike *Tales of a Low-Rent Birder,* whose essays were lifted from the pages of the "Peregrine Observer" newsletter, the stories collected here do not know a common origin. Ten were originally written for "The Catbird Seat," which appears in Cornell's *Living Bird Quarterly.* Nine were drawn from my *New York Times* column, "In the Natural State" (several of these were reprinted in *Bird Watcher's Digest*). Four herald from the "American Birding" pages of *American Birds,* and one (an uncolumned essay) was first published in *Birder's World.* These columns differ somewhat in focus and style, though only a writer might see this (and only an editor might care).

Before letting you, the reader, move on to the balance of the book, I ask that you indulge a writer for a few more lines. There are several people whose efforts served to make the stories you are about to read more enjoyable and you should know who they are. These people are editors, *good* editors—

the kind that make writers read better than their natural talents provide.

So saying, I would like to thank Susan Drennan of *American Birds,* Rick Bonney, Jill Crane, and Tim Gallagher of *Living Bird Quarterly,* Eldon Greij of *Birder's World,* and Richard Roberts, Fletcher Roberts, and Bob Stock of the *New York Times* for their fine, fine efforts. They do their profession proud.

Pete Dunne
Cape May Point, N.J.
May 1993

MORE TALES OF A LOW-RENT BIRDER

Keith Hansen 1993

A Golden Plover at Ebb Tide

The bird was crouched in a shallow depression above the reach of the morning tide, on the beach that linked the two towns. A casual stroller would never have seen it. Even a very attentive passerby, one skilled at sifting sand-colored birds from sand, could not have been certain (so well did the bird blend in with her surroundings). If the bird remained very still, there was nothing to distinguish her from the darker patches of sand. And the bird remained *very* still. This was the second most important day in her young life. This was the day she would die.

Her life had begun on a bluff rich with flowers that fell sharply into the Arctic Ocean. To her left, the channels of the Mackenzie River delta shimmered like a web of silver. Overhead, Snow Buntings spiraled and the shadows of jaegers haunted the earth. But the first thing the plover had seen when she opened her eyes (*before she was three minutes old),* was the gray arctic sea.

A writer would find this significant: the fact that the bird would begin and end her life within sight of two oceans thousands of miles apart—but it would mean nothing to the bird. Her mind had no gift for recalling places and events outside of immediate time and need, the thing we call memory. In the orbit of her existence, the bluff and its carpet of flowers were four months behind (or six months ahead). If her fortune were different, the knowledge of the place and its significance would awaken in her when it was time—on some day in May during a spring that she would never see.

Right now, the incredible mechanism that was her brain told her that it was time to migrate. It told her how she should do this, what route she should take, and, ultimately, it would tell her when and where to stop. Even now, dying, the brain said *"south,"* so this was the direction she faced, her head drawn back, eyes closed, the tip of the wing that had been injured barely touching the sand.

Migration is a time of great stress and peril for birds and the inherent dangers are magnified by inexperience. Only a fraction of the birds born in any given year survive to maturity—harsh terms by human standards. Migration is the first major cut in the ranks of birds and survival depends as much upon innate skills as it does upon finding places en route to rest and feed.

Unfortunately, the migratory way stations birds depend upon are being usurped to meet the habitat needs of a more aggressive species—our species. Forests are cut, wetlands filled, beaches bulkheaded to protect houses—exacerbating the problem of erosion and destroying the beach.

We compound the difficulties of migration by erecting barriers—glass-encased structures that treacherously reflect the sky, relay towers anchored by webs knit of steel that are invisible to birds at night. Many hundreds of millions of birds collide with structures made by humans every year and die.

Every year, because of human activities, migration becomes just a little bit more perilous. And every year, fewer and fewer birds make the cut.

But *our* bird's injury was an accident, a near brush with an ancient enemy—a Peregrine Falcon—that claimed the life of another plover feeding nearby. Though she was not the intended prey, the hard leading edge of the falcon's wing struck our young plover's wing as the falcon cut through the panicked flock. Two of the very fine bones near the end of the wing were broken.

The bird could still fly, but not as well as a golden plover should. When the flocks departed on the last day of August to begin their great journey south, she remained. Three healing weeks passed and though her wing was not fully mended the changing season would let her wait no longer. She left the Arctic on a morning with the air filled with snow and migrating sea ducks.

Flying alone, without other birds to take their turn breaking trail, she used energy quickly and friction dragged at her wings. She tried flying with several species of waterfowl but their speed was not her speed.

More wing-weary than exhausted, the bird put down in a newly harvested wheat field in northern Manitoba. The place offered grasshoppers made torpid by the deepening cold and it offered company. Two days after she arrived, she was joined by two other plovers, juveniles like herself. One bird had a broken leg. In a week, when they left, she joined them. Though her wing was imperfectly mended and energy reserves were still insufficient, her need for company was great.

Flying as three was easier than flying solo, but the bad wing was still very much a handicap and it sapped her energy quickly. Over northern Maine, she dropped back and pitched into a potato field. Strangely, the other plovers joined her. A bond had been formed. They were a team. But food was not plentiful. The growing cold was driving the worms they sought beyond the reach of their bills. Two days later, the threesome took wing again, heading south and east—leaving the coast behind.

The great storm that forced them to make landfall on an island off the coast of Massachusetts lasted two punishing days. During that time, the birds huddled under a sandy lip on the lee side of a grassy knoll. They spent the week following the storm searching the short-cut grass for the food they desperately needed (avoiding as best they could grounds keepers and men who moved about in motorized carts).

Food was not particularly plentiful. The season was late and golf club grounds keepers wage a ferocious war against insects that might mar a fairway. When the two birds that were her companions lifted off, the injured bird hesitated. Her strength was still not the measure of theirs. Locked in her brain was the number of miles that lay ahead and the same brain told her that her fuel, the layers of fat she had amassed, was not sufficient. She stood on the open fairway and watched.

The pair climbed quickly, purposefully—cleaving the air

with scimitar wings, putting the continent behind. One of the birds called back to their stranded companion—a low, plaintive whistle that she answered immediately. The pair circled once, maybe to get their bearings, maybe to offer encouragement. When they lined out this time, out over the open waters of the Atlantic, she followed.

For several hours she managed to hold the hemisphere-crossing pace but slowly her energy played out. Land, she knew, lay somewhere to the west. She fell behind, trailed the pair for a time, and then turned away, heading west. It took eight hours fighting a northwest head wind before she found the land she sought.

As her strength waned, she lost altitude until her wings barely cleared the water. Twice, waves nearly claimed her. Once, she actually landed on the water. But plovers are not phalaropes. They are not made to float. She had no choice but to continue. No choice at all.

She reached the beach at the very tip of New Jersey just before dawn—a small bit of fortune. Had she arrived an hour later the sharp-eyed gulls would have driven her into the water and fought for her remains. The exhausted bird collapsed just above the reach of the cresting tide and was asleep immediately.

She awoke near midmorning, stood, and moved unsteadily toward the water's edge. Earlier in the season, she might have hunted more successfully, but the cold air had already driven most of the temperature-sensitive worms deeper. A constant stream of strollers kept the bird moving, distracting her, forcing her to use energy she didn't have just avoiding their feet.

Frustrated, the bird flew to the other side of the dunes where a grassy, well-pooled meadow lay. She explored the shallows for insects. But the meadow had been repeatedly treated to control mosquitoes, leaving little for birds to eat. Most migrating shorebirds stayed only a few minutes before flying on in search of more productive areas but flight was beyond the plover's capacity. Returning to the beach she crouched in a shallow depression above the tide and the heaviest pedestrian traffic. This is where she spent the rest of the day and, after the sun fell, the night.

When morning came, she remained where she was. There was no energy left to search for the food that might have sustained her. What was left of her life would be measured in hours.

That afternoon, a young couple enjoying the last days of Indian summer came down the beach accompanied by a large red setter. Though the dog was supposed to be on a leash, few people paid attention to the regulation. The couple walked within twenty feet of the bird without seeing her. Even the coursing setter missed her the first time, but on the return trip the dog nearly tripped over the huddled form.

The bird felt the dog's nose move over her back. She tried to stand but could not. With an effort she succeeded in opening her eyes. In front of her, to the south, was the sea.

The dog ran down the beach at full gallop, eager to show its prize, nearly bowling the woman over in its excitement.

"What do you have there, Loki?" the man demanded. "Hold up, damn it! Let me see. Stop!" With incredible effort, the dog managed to immobilize its fore end (but the hindquarters were simply out of control).

"Oh, my God!" the woman exclaimed, horrified. "It's a dead bird. A dirty old dead bird. Drop it," she commanded, dealing Loki a sharp slap on the nose. "Drop it!"

Loki dropped it.

The afternoon sun spread a golden wash over the still form, making its underparts glow. Even now, it was beautiful.

"Huh. I wonder what kind of bird it is," the man mused aloud. "It's not a sea gull."

"It's a dead one," his companion said impatiently, as she stepped in front of Loki, whose interest in the bird was unabated. "Come on," she demanded. "Let's get away from here before he picks it up again. It probably has some kind of disease."

An hour later, a wave propelled by the incoming tide claimed the bird and carried it into Delaware Bay.

Twenty-four hundred miles to the south, a single golden plover landed on a shallow, tidal flat surrounded by mangroves and proceeded to feed, clumsily because of its exhaustion and because of its broken leg.

Hansen
1993

Silver and Gold for Josephine

The old railroad tracks leading from "the Beanery" to the bay were unused and overgrown. There wasn't room to walk abreast so we navigated single file—wife Linda, the shortest, up front; friend Pete Bacinski behind. I claimed the spot in the middle.

The three of us were on a quest. We had risen early and driven far. We had planned this venture days in advance and had refused to allow any last-minute trappings to stand in the way of our ambition.

We were searching for an incomparable creature—a bird whose wings and tail are the color of silver in moonlight and whose head and body seem cast from molten gold. The eyes, bill, and legs are black. Jet black.

But if you are not, yourself, a bird watcher you may be wondering why three mature adults would go to the trouble of searching for this bird. You may be wondering if it is valuable. Wondering if it was lost or stolen. Curious to know if there was a prize or reward if we found it.

This is going to take a bit of explanation. These questions unlock a door that opens to a maze of complicated answers—many of them nearly correct. Bird watchers take the impetus for their actions so much for granted, and we sometimes forget that those who do not share our passion do not understand our motives either.

The *excuse* for seeking this particular bird was that Linda had never seen one before. The bird with the silver wings and golden body is a southern species, a bird of dark hardwood swamps. The northern limit of its range traces its edge somewhere through New Jersey, my native state, and although Linda has seen and enjoyed over five hundred species of North American birds, the vantage offered by her years of western residency had not placed this special prize within her reach.

For Linda, it would be a Life Bird.

That explains Linda's interest. As for Pete Bacinski, it would be a "year bird," meaning that although he'd seen this bird before, he hadn't yet laid eyes on one this year.

If you truly are not a birder, I know that this must sound a trifle contrived. After all, to carry this line of reasoning to an extreme, it could be argued that he'd never seen the bird while standing on one leg, or while brushing his teeth either, and what possible difference can it make?

As I said, this was just an excuse. It doesn't even come close to offering a reason. But sometimes even birders need an excuse to motivate us to do something—even something we really want to do in the first place.

For my part, I'd seen the bird of silver and gold many times, in fact, seen the very individual we were searching for just three days earlier. What excuse did I have for joining the quest? None whatsoever. I was motivated by something much better than an excuse—a gift of insight given to me by a woman with bird-black eyes and an open mind. I had a *reason.* I was searching for the bird of silver and gold because the bird is *beautiful.*

There. I think that states it plainly enough. The bird is beautiful and people derive pleasure from beautiful things, be they cars, sweaters, paintings, sunsets, wallpaper, or rings.

Or rings.

She told me her name was Josephine. She clipped each syllable and the smile that formed the last part of her name remained on her face. "Welcome to Maralal," she said. I thanked her and began filling out guest cards for the members of our Kenya tour group.

While I wrote we chatted. Her English was halting but good. She offered, without being asked, the information most often sought by tour leaders: when the animals were coming down to drink at the watering hole, whether the leopards were coming regularly to the bait, and so forth.

I thanked her and asked about the birds around the lodge. She couldn't tell me very much and I could tell that what I'd asked wasn't a question commonly posed at Maralal. But if it did not elicit much information, the question did invite her curiosity.

"Why you wish to know about birds?" she asked.

"To watch them," I explained.

"You come to Kenya from United States to see birds?"

"Yes."

"But why you watch birds?" she asked. The question was open, honest, and sincere—free of the subtle tone of derision or condescension that I have come to associate with it. Josephine was genuinely curious and all she asked was for me to tell her the truth.

In the process, she stumped a wordsmith at his craft. Though I have dealt with this question a million times, in dozens of essays and thousands of conversations, I suddenly realized that I had never given it the benefit of the truth. Most people who pose this question want only an excuse, something easily dismissed, something that doesn't have to be taken seriously because *they,* in their narrow-mindedness, do not care to take birds seriously.

Nobody, until Josephine, had ever wanted the truth, and until that moment, I had never been motivated to forge the truth into words.

As she waited, as I groped for an explanation that would carry the full weight of truth to this person, I noticed her hands. Her hands were bejeweled with an assortment of rings. Beautiful rings! And every finger, it seemed, hosted at least one. Some were gold, some silver; all were finely crafted. A few may have held stones, but most seemed unadorned except for the artistry captured in their intricate forms. Against the dark backdrop of her hand, they sparkled and flared.

"You have many beautiful rings," I said.

"Thank you," she said, puzzled by the digression.

"They make you happy, these rings?" I asked.

"Yes," she said again.

"The birds I look for are like the rings, then," I explained. "They are beautiful and they make me happy, but I cannot collect them on my fingers so I collect them only in my mind."

Josephine laughed, delighted with the explanation.

We ambled down the old railroad bed, past fresh plowed fields and woodlots flush with spring. We stopped, now and again, to identify and enjoy this bird or that. We met friends along the way, fellow treasure hunters returning from quests of their own.

We asked of their fortune and they obliged—recounting for us the prizes their skill and fortune had snared (mostly semi-precious songsters like Ruby-crowned Kinglets and Yellow-rumped Warblers). One lucky treasure hunter, however, had found a Pearl of Great Price, a Kentucky Warbler. Nobody mentioned the bird that was the objective of our quest.

The old rail bed entered a tunnel of trees. The ground grew wet, then spongy, then disappeared beneath still, dark water. High overhead, where the world still bathed in sunlight, migrating warblers chased insects through the foliage of spring. But beneath the canopy, between the rails, it was dark and tranquil.

We stopped. Stood. Waited.

Nothing.

We tried imitating the bird's loud, ringing call to elicit a response.

Nothing again.

We tried imitating a screech owl to incite the ire of the bird. Still nothing. Having run out of options, we simply waited.

Sometimes quests are successful—and that's birding. Sometimes quests are unsuccessful—and that's birding, too. But quests that are transformed into published stories are almost always successful and this story won't disappoint you.

We had decided to leave. We were, in fact, in the process of leaving and thoughts of lunch at a favorite spot in town were already crowding the disappointment from our minds when the bird that was the object of our quest broke the silence and the suspense.

"Sweet, sweet, sweet, sweet, sweet."

The song was a good deal softer than any of us expected. It lacked the bright ringing quality the bird is famous for, but it was unmistakable. We hurried back along the tracks to a spot well beyond the place where we'd kept our vigil.

One minute passed . . . two . . . and then, there it was! Fifty feet away, foraging along the edge of a dark, peaty bank, the bird of silver and gold—a Prothonotary Warbler.

It stepped from the shadows into a circle of sunlight. It threw back its head and sang again, making our ears ring. By branch and tussock, it moved in our direction—searching for insects, oblivious to our interest. Forty feet . . . thirty . . . twenty . . . fifteen . . .

Something at the water's edge, *at our feet,* caught its eye. The bird launched itself and landed too close for binoculars to be brought to bear. It maneuvered among the branches, navigated a course around our legs, accepted our scrutiny until the image of the bird was lodged firmly and forever in the coffers of our minds.

Linda was elated. Pete was pleased. Me? I was happy, too—happy beyond reason. Except I wish that Josephine could have been there because I think that she would have enjoyed seeing this bird that sparkled like the rings on her fingers. If not Josephine, then any one of the million people who have ever asked me why I watch birds.

Birder or Bag Lady?

It looked like reveille, like Dunkirk, like a druid sunrise service. Try to picture it: four hundred British birders flanking a wet hedge all draped in identical oilskin jackets; all shod in regulation Wellies; all adorned with German optics. I was impressed. A similar number of American birders wouldn't wear anything more universal than bored expressions.

The sage-colored assemblage, patiently waiting for some skulking, feathered miscreant, would have been the picture of uniformity except for one magnificent incongruity. Deep in the rear ranks was a single splash of color—a robin's-egg blue (i.e., American Robin) Gortex jacket. The parka, it turned out, was worn by another "Yank" birder named Mindy. Mindy was from Indiana. She couldn't, she explained, find any birders in the United States so she came to the U.K. for company. She said this with a straight face.

If Mindy was imprinted on waxed cotton jackets, I can understand how she failed to find any birders in places like Point Pelee in May and Cape May Point in September, but this brings up a good point. Birding garb here in the colonies is pretty eclectic. There is nothing that might be called the universal birding uniform, nothing that distinguishes birders from society's rank and file.

There are birders who look as if they were cut right out of an Eddie Bauer catalogue and birders who look as if they were cut down from a garden stake overlooking the peas. There are birders who dress like part of an Everest assault team and birders who dress like penitents with ten years to run on a thirty-year sentence. Take away their binoculars and how *would* you know a birder if you saw one? How would you distinguish a birder from, say, a bag lady?

"Are you kidding me?" my friend Patty observed. "You can pick out a birder a mile away." Patty is a waitress in Cape May, New Jersey, and since birders are notoriously lousy tippers, it is incumbent upon waitresses to recognize them on sight.

"OK," I said, sipping grandly from a frosted mug, "you tell me. How can you distinguish birders from regular patrons?"

"Well, first, birders wear outlandish hats and they never take them off when they go indoors."

"Huh," I said into my mug, suddenly conscious of the CMBO visor festooned with American Birding Association convention pins that was perched on my noggin. "What else?"

"And they drink cheap beer or straight liquor. All the tourists drink piña coladas, pink squirrels, grasshoppers, or strawberry daiquiris."

"Or wine," I said defensively (wondering what the hell a pink squirrel was). "Sometimes we drink wine."

"Or wine," Patty admitted. "House wine. By the glass. And they always ask the price. If a birder is wearing a jacket, they drape it over a chair or just let it fall on the floor—*never* hang them up. Half the time they don't even take them off."

"Nonbirders don't ever keep their jackets on?" I challenged.

"Well, if they do," Patty replied, "nonbirders have started wearing jackets that look like quilts stitched out of bird club patches. Cripes, I've seen double-sashed Girl Scouts sporting fewer badges than some of the birders who wander in here."

"OK, OK," I soothed. "What about the rest of it? Shoes? Pants?"

"Scuffed Rockports or running shoes," she replied unhesitantly. "Beige slacks or jeans. The slacks and Rockports are a combination; so are the runners and jeans. There's never any crossing over."

She hesitated a moment, thinking hard. "No designer jeans," she added, "and most of the denim looks like it's spent half its life on a towel rack in some gas station restroom. The laces on the running shoes have been spliced several times. You can see toes on at least one foot."

"And," she added, "it's a good thing birds can't smell. Most of the sneakers are so ripe they could curl the whiskers on a sewer rat."

"Ha!" I challenged. "By that description, how would you distinguish a birder from a bag lady? From a bum?"

Patty reared up over the bar like a lioness over a kill. "Because," she shouted triumphantly, "bag ladies carry all their stuff in bags. Birders cram all their junk into a couple of dozen pockets and pouches hanging off their belts."

"No camouflaged fatigue pants?" I inquired cautiously.

"Uh-uh," Patty said. "Too stylish."

"Jewelry?"

"The women? Never."

"Well," I said, grudgingly convinced, "I guess you can pick 'em out all right."

"Want another?" she said, indicating the mug.

"No thanks," I said, reaching into my pocket and depositing a measured amount of U.S. coinage next to my empty plate.

Patty stared solemnly at the meager tithing and shook her head. "Yep," she affirmed, "you're a birder all right."

Homecoming, Coon Ridge

There was one car in the lot, about right for midweek and south winds. Come the weekend or a cold front and late-arriving hawk watchers find themselves parking on the grass. I pulled up, claimed a space, slipped into a day pack, and with no more than a glance back down the lane, started for the trail head that leads to the crest of the ridge.

How many times did I stand in that lot, waiting for the man in the fire-engine red jeep to draw to a stop?

I don't know. Dozens of times. Scores.

How many times did I jump to the passenger door, eager to fall under the spell of his words, eager to "get up top," and stand next to the Master while the river of raptors flowed around us?

It's impossible to say. The particulars have been eroded by time. His words and the birds and great moments that marked the path of my discovery . . . and our friendship . . . have run together in a blur. What I recall is his hawk-like visage. A flowing mane of hair, a billowing beard, and eyes that never admitted that there was such a thing as age.

Most of all, I remember his voice. It was sonorous and deep, rising and falling with a tumble of words that flowed like water. Why, if William Jennings Bryan had possessed the voice of Floyd P. Wolfarth, he could have called himself an orator.

Long an insider's secret, Raccoon Ridge—*Coon Ridge*—has slipped its gag; the location of this New Jersey hawk-watch site and its fame have fallen into the pool of common knowledge. No, the place is not Hawk Mountain—not in elevation, not in popularity, perhaps not even in the magnitude of its flight. But the great wall of stone that supports Coon is the same "endless mountain" of the Lenapi Indians that Hawk Mountain Sanctuary straddles. And the legacy of Coon Ridge is just as proud, almost as long, and . . .

It was a *secret!* A secret known only to the members of the Urner Ornithological Club and a handful of carefully chosen confederates. Even the name of the place was intended to confound hawk shooters, and the shroud of secrecy surrounding the location of Coon survived long after the guns were silenced.

In time, the secret took on the character of a barrier, a threshold. To be ken to Coon was to be a member of North Jersey birding's inner circle, a member of the clan. And before Donald Heintzelman spilled the gruel in his *Autumn Hawk Flights,* before the publication of Bill Boyle's *Bird Finding in New Jersey,* there was only one way to cross the threshold. Someone in the inner circle had to reach out and usher you across.

Somberly hooded juncos fled the road. The mountain laurels whispered among themselves and drew back. A mourning cloak butterfly that had survived the season's first hard frost reeled drunkenly through the trees. I considered taking the shortcut, for old time's sake, but kept to the road instead. The shortcut was for younger men.

"Four hundred years old if it's a day," Floyd would intone as his spunky jeep bounced and churned up the path, navigating switchbacks and sidestepping rocks that reach for oil pans. "Four hundred years, this road. Built by hand. Ah, those were real men in those days," he'd pronounce (by which he meant that their like are not to be found today).

No, they don't build men like those old Dutch copper miners who once hauled ox carts of ore over Kaiser Road. And they don't build 'em like the old teamster from Nutley, New Jersey, Floyd P. Wolfarth, a man who knew Charles Urner and Lee Edwards and was a founding member of the Urner Ornithological Club. *Floyd Wolfarth,* who saw ten thousand pintails in Hatfield Swamp . . . picked a Mew Gull out of thin air at Newburyport, Mass. . . . founded the Boonton Christmas Bird Count . . . and who birded with "the Great Man," Roger Peterson, in the Hackensack Meadows before half the birders alive today were sucking bottles of formula.

The road gets steeper after the first switchback, the rocks bolder. The rain has knocked the color out of the hillsides. Only the poplar leaves still hold their branches, crowning the hillsides with gold. The oak leaves have shivered their way to the ground, covering Kaiser Road with a coarse brown shroud. They are slippery, making the footing treacherous. Gravity sucks on the heels of boots, making calves twitch. Soon the twitch will become an ache, and then an agony.

There was a time when I used to climb this track in something under thirty minutes. My record was eighteen and I ran. But that was before the invention of cholesterol, during an age when knees bent without protest. It was long ago. Now, more than ever, I listen for the rumble of Floyd's jeep coming up from behind. But that is a sound that these Kittatinny hillsides have not heard for many years—and will never hear again.

Every summer, in the shadow of another wall of stone, this one in Portal, Arizona, it is my privilege to help Victor Emanuel with his Camp Chiricahua—a birding camp for high-school-age students. Every day is filled with discovery. Every night is an occasion for spirited conversation. And on those long drives connecting southeast Arizona's scattered hot spots, the essence of birding is held to the light and every facet discussed.

It was on one of those drives that I stumbled upon the word that drew so much of birding into focus—a single catalytic word. That word is "tribal." Birding is tribal.

Think about it. Birders form a separate society, a subculture, a tribe, and a subculture erects barriers between those who share a common interest and those who do not. This barrier is enforced by an esoteric language, patterns of interaction, modes of dress.

Birding has its own mores, like its ethic of honesty. It has its rituals, like the Big Day and the Christmas Bird Count. But more than these, birding enjoys one key attribute that is eminently tribal. Birding reveres its elders—the lore masters, the great teachers.

Many, if not most birders, can trace their interest and their development to one special person who took them under a wing. Who taught them the skills and the lore. Who initiated them into the fabric of birding society.

This mentor and pupil bond is key to birding, maybe irreplaceable. It helped make birding what it is. It serves to hold it together. And it guides us as we navigate a course through an uncertain future.

The jeep would grind to a halt where the road crossed the Appalachian Trail. Floyd would amble to the rear of the car and draw forth his gear with the care of a surgeon laying out his instruments. He ambled more than walked (though Floyd always insisted that it was a "limp").

"An old injury," he'd explain. "Tendon crushed by a thousand [sometimes 'ten thousand'] pounds [occasionally 'tons'] of steel" that had somehow fallen from the bed of his truck. Floyd was never one to let something like particulars stand in the way of a good story.

Binoculars in one hand, stuffed owl and lounge chair in the other, he'd "limp" toward the spot on the ridge that was his by decree and deference. Then, unfettered of his burdens, he'd draw himself erect and face the wind.

"Ah," he would pronounce. "This is magNIFICENT." "MAAAGnificent," he'd repeat and his voice was so full of command that even God-in-Heaven probably glanced down to see what He'd done that had impressed Old Wolfarth so deeply.

"They'll be coming beak to tail on this wind," Floyd would promise. "Beak to tail." Then, having said all that needed to be said, he'd walk the piece of carrion he charitably called a stuffed owl down to a carefully hidden pole and battle to lever his lure aloft. Sometimes Floyd won, sometimes the owl, and in retrospect, it occurs to me that the only thing that could get the better of Floyd in a war of wills was that decrepit bird.

It was the Boy Scouts of America that turned Floyd's mind and many other young minds toward the natural world and to birding. This was the Boy Scouts that taught woodcraft, and chivalry . . . *not* the organization that sells off its land holdings to pay its bills that conservationists know today. And birders of that age were also brought to the wonder of birds in grammar schools—through teachers who had love and wisdom to spare; through bread crumbs scattered on window sills; and later, by leaflets sent through the mail by the National Audubon Society.

But we live in another age now. The ranks of Boy Scouts have thinned, and in schools "nature study" has been supplanted by "environmental studies" that focus on "pollution," "solid waste," and "ozone depletion." Children go home right after school and they are ordered to stay inside because the world is no longer safe. Woodlands are places of menace.

More and more, new birders seem drawn from the ranks of colleges. Mentors are college profs or experienced birders who teach adult education courses. And the last three decades have seen the proliferation of professional mentors, bird tour leaders—who carry the banners of VENT, Wings, and Field Guides, Inc. (and the admiration of all who follow them). Their skills are the stuff of legend and their followers recount their exploits with pride.

Having battled the elements to a near draw, Wolfarth would return to his mount and pin his eyes to the sky. The great Kittatinny Ridge had been brushed by his gaze (and 300,000 years of ice, wind, and rain) for so long that the peaks had been eroded to bumps—bumps with names like "the Nob,"

"Catfish," and "Stigs." No hawk could remain anonymous for long when Wolfarth scanned the skies.

Distant Red-taileds flashed secret signals that only his eyes could read. Cooper's Hawks whose tails failed to pass muster were too ashamed to show their faces when Floyd stood at his post.

And when that oh-so-insignificant black dot would appear on the horizon—so far away that lesser eyes dismissed it as "only another Turkey Vulture"—it was Wolfarth who brought us to attention.

"Watch this bird," he'd command. "Watch it! This," he'd rumble, "is going to be something GOOD!"

In this age of video, and magazines, and newsletters and bird finder guides and hot lines and computer bulletin boards, the personal bond that forms between a master and his apprentice is still very much a part of birding. It takes a special person. It takes a bond. It takes a pair. *This* is what it takes to make birders and imbue them with the wisdom and ethics of the tribe.

And then one day, the bond is broken. And every birder becomes a vessel of the past and an emissary to the future. Thus is our tradition preserved.

I reached the top in something over thirty minutes. The winds were right. The time was right. Only the solitude felt wrong.

The bird was fairly close before I saw it, almost naked-eye close—a stealth raptor, offering a head-on profile that deflected all mortal efforts to pin a name upon it.

But something about this bird makes you hold your glass on it long after the point of comfort. There is something about this bird that makes your throat close, that shuts out the world so that all reality draws down to two points and a single line.

The bird was like the man who used to stand on this ridge beside me—steady, unwavering, larger than life.

"Watch this bird," a voice buried deep in my conscious

counseled. "Watch this bird. This is going to be something good."

"I'm watching it, Floyd," I thought.

"Big. Am I right?"

"Yes, big."

"Holds the ridge like it was bolted there."

"Uh-huh."

"I think you've got it. Yes, sir," the echo of an echo of a voice shouted from some unbridgeable distance, *"had it all the way."* Which is flattering, but not quite true. It is more accurate to say I had it *half* way.

And the bird, the young Golden Eagle, left the ridge, taking a course that offered easier passage. I left too, but before I did, I ambled down the north slope a little way. There, a stone's throw from the place that Wolfarth once held forth, there is a tiny cairn made of Kittatinny stone, and a handmade wooden cross. As has become my habit, I added another stone to the pile. Then started on down.

Keith Hansen 1993

The Song of Killing

The anger in the western sky diminished until heaven and earth were knit by a red and violet scar. The neutral fog crept out of its hiding place, filling woodland hollows with murk and the air with the sour tang of fallen leaves.

In the leaves, two mice, or maybe voles, argued over some runway right-of-way. Their squeaked objections, faint and few at first, grew louder in measure with their failure and growing frustration. The harangue reached deep into the night and fell upon many ears, kindling interest in some, indifference in others. It drew, finally, from some dark corner of the universe, a shadow.

How to describe this thing? The way it seems, or the way it appears? The creature that truly is, or the creature our fear makes it? In daylight a descriptive accounting would be no challenge at all. Sunlight would reveal a large, stolid bird cloaked in the colors of winter woodlands—grays, browns, and cold ocher. Set atop its head are the devil's own horns. Set within staring circles, eyes of sleepy malice. Its wings are broad and rounded and silent as a feather in free fall. Its bill is cruelly hooked and its feet a net of talons. Yes, this is how the creature appears in daylight—a powerful bird, but one tethered to shadows and made sport of by crows. But at night, the bird's powers wax and it becomes a thing of terror. In forests and parks, across open fields and suburban woodlots, it spreads its wings and sallies forth—to hunt for the living, to punish the incautious, and to sing the song of killing.

What is the song of killing? It is an ancient thing. Some say it is older than life; some say no. Some say it is just the shadow cast by life; others, that it is the dark ocean that all life swims in. None among the living have standing to say.

The killing song is not even a song—at least not as you and I think of songs—because it has none of the properties of sound. The killing song is more akin to a memory that stalks at the edge of recall, a silent hum to a nameless tune whose words you cannot remember.

But if the killing song *were* a song, and if it *did* have the properties of sound, it might approximate the noise a piano makes when the notes on opposing ends of the keyboard are struck simultaneously. If you wait until the enjoined notes fade and fail and become an echo trapped in memory, at this moment, you can almost hear the silent strains of the killing song.

If the killing song were a smell (instead of a song), it might recall many things. The sweet smell of rot; the musty smell of snakes; the sad smell of marigolds trampled into newly spaded earth. But these smells would only suggest themselves. The killing song (if any living person could truly smell a song) would be more akin to the odor of windows in the rain, the scent of orchids across an empty room, and the smell of ice so cold it numbs the mind.

But the killing song cannot be smelled, because songs have no smell. It cannot be heard except, perhaps, by those creatures that sing it. The killing song is something wild creatures sense. And humans? Yes. Barely.

You have felt it, too. On a lonely country road. Late at night. When the shadows close in. The air goes chill. And the hairs on the back of your neck tingle as your feet know sudden speed. Imagination? Oh, no! You have been brushed by the killing song.

You have felt it at home, alone. While reading a book, beneath the light of a single lamp. Out of the corner of your eye you catch a movement—in the corner that even morning sunlight avoids. And you look up quickly—to stare into an empty corner.

Only later, after you return to a brighter, better-lit room with your freshly brewed tea, do you realize that you are humming to yourself and the tune has no words you can recall.

The shadow swept across the winter landscape as silent as a memory. It took a perch on the limb of a slumbering oak, and if oaks dream, then this tree's dreams turned ugly enough to be recalled when sap flowed later that spring.

The mice (or voles) felt the killing song sweep over, and the feud was momentarily forgotten. Their silence was utter, and if they could have quieted their hearts, they would have done this too. Moments turned to minutes and minutes passed. The killing song did not sweep their lives away and gradually the horror of it diminished.

Neither rodent knew whether this meant that the song had gone elsewhere or whether a moment's incaution would sing them into oblivion. Neither was willing to put it to the test, not yet. So they waited.

The dark lump of a bird who was the vessel of the killing song also waited. The bird could have moved on, taking the song elsewhere. But the night was young; the song momentarily suspended, not done. There is plenty of time in a winter night for singing the killing song, so the bird waited, biding its time, trusting the power of the song and its capacity to sing to the death when fortune inclined.

Perhaps you think that the bird is cruel. No, it is not—no crueler than the song.

Perhaps you think that the killing song should be banned, that no creatures should be allowed, wittingly or unwittingly, to sing other creatures into a silence they would not choose for themselves?

You might just as well, and just as easily, ban life. The only way to stop the killing song is to destroy the audience that supports it.

Some who defend the creatures that sing the killing song do so by explaining that there is no malice, after all. These feathered (and furred, and scaled) sirens are just "products of evolution," they say. These creatures "fill an important niche." And "maintain the balance." And "insure the health and stability of prey population," they maintain. The bird that sings the killing song sings only for its supper.

Excuse me, but I am not inclined to sing the party line. I refuse to believe that creatures that sing the killing song do so merely to survive, that evolution has molded creatures to sing efficiently but with no more feeling than a toaster browning an English muffin. I refuse.

I am more inclined to believe that a creature that sings with such authority and finesse is in harmony with the song and relishes the cold heat of it. I find this far easier to accept than the notion that death is dealt out, night after night after night, all over the planet, with cold, mechanical indifference. That those creatures that sing the killing song and those creatures that are seduced by it are bound by no greater bond than hunger, or habit, or the twitch of a nerve.

I believe that creatures that sing the song of killing sing in concert with great forces—forces that bind and unbind the poles of the universe. And I believe, because I cannot know, that when the song passes through them it vibrates with feelings that run deeper than their understanding or mine.

The mice (or voles) grew impatient in time. Their dispute was unsettled and their small brains could find no way to resolve it, except by retreat, and neither was willing to accept this.

Soon the dispute became vocal once again. Then it became physical. The sound of the killing song grew louder, but they ignored it. The song grew so loud that it became a physical presence so real that it eclipsed their own.

The embattled rodents heard, felt, and saw nothing. One minute they were locked in combat, the next they were not. They had become part of a sound that smelled like ice and hung in the universe like a red and violet note struck on an invisible keyboard.

Only the owl heard the dying echoes of the song and, although it was hungry and wanted to feed, it waited—out of respect, or perhaps for its pleasure—until the song had passed into silence.

It Must Be Love

He was the only figure seated at the bar, a man in his early forties wearing an Explorer's Inn T-shirt and binoculars slung bandolier fashion under an arm. He raised a glass to his mouth and tipped it back, stopping the ice cubes with his teeth. The glass was empty.

"Not a happy man," the bartender thought of his patron. "A political exile perhaps. More likely a man coming to grips with a love gone bad."

"Another, sir?" the bartender invited.

"One more," the solitary figure agreed, forgetting that that was what he'd said the last time. The drink arrived and the patron grasped it with two hands but he did not drink right away. Instead he stared down at the discolored contents.

Yes, once he had been a happy man, a birder (and this is the happiest thing that a person could ever hope to be). Once, he'd wasted whole, wonderful weekends wandering through woodlands, watching whatever came his way.

"A damn good birder," he thought to the glass and to himself and it was true. But those happy, carefree days were gone. Gone half a lifetime. Lost to an age when the fifth American Redstart of the day still brought smiles and a rumbling tummy didn't stop a day's birding (because there was only one tummy to rumble, his, so it didn't matter).

"Back before I became a tour leader," he thought, raising the glass and draining it. He didn't even notice when the bartender replaced his empty glass with a full one.

"It happened before I knew it," he thought and this too was true. There he'd been, just a shy, quiet person who liked watching birds, just one of the happy tag-along members of the local bird club on the Saturday morning field trips.

Then he began beating the field trip leaders to calls. And finding saw-whet owls on Christmas Bird Counts. And reading off five minutes' worth of local sightings at every bird club meeting. And getting his initials plastered all over the regional accounts in *American Birds*—sometimes even his whole name!

And *then* came that fateful day when he showed up for a scheduled field trip and the appointed leader did not! And nobody knew what to do. And then everyone turned to him, the bright new star.

The next thing he knew, *he*, the quiet, shy person, was at the head of a line of twenty people and every one of them was depending on him to know which way to turn at trail junctions, how to tell the difference between Blackpoll and Bay-breasted warblers, when to call a pit stop.

Suddenly, *he* was the one who had to make sure everyone got on the bird, had to shush people for being too noisy, had to act aloof and confident (when all he really wanted to do was just watch birds and have fun).

He didn't blow a call all day. And it *really* wasn't fair to take him to task for being several hours late getting to the restrooms. After all, he was still too young to drink coffee. But after he found the Black-billed Cuckoo everyone forgot about his strategic indiscretion.

Well, almost everyone.

After the trip, (almost) everyone said "thank you" and "good job." Pretty soon, he was just a little less shy and he was leading one-day field trips every weekend. Then he began organizing holiday weekend road trips. Then he was planning and leading club tours to places like southeast Arizona and the Rio Grande Valley.

And then, one day, the director of one of the big national bird tour companies had called and invited him to co-lead a tour that would include local hot spots. For pay! And he'd snapped at the chance. Gone for it like a young kingbird goes for a passing monarch butterfly.

"And I was hooked," he said aloud to the glass.

That was many years ago, now. Many years and many tours and many hundreds of tour participants.

Now, he was a professional field trip leader, a person whose job it was to find exotic birds and make people happy. His days were long, filled with big decisions and tiny birds that never sit long enough on a branch. His nights were spent checking airline reservations, arranging for local guides, ordering box lunches (some with, some without mayonnaise/luncheon meat/pork products/cucumbers/MSG/etc.), and staring at the ceilings of his motel rooms, wondering whether to try for the Lammergeier again tomorrow. Or whether to just blow it off and head directly for the Mara.

He sighed.

"Another drink, Bwana," the bartender coaxed.

"No, thank you," the leader said, glancing at his watch, draining his glass. He paid the check and headed for the door, the taste of sugar-beet sweetened Coke still thick in his mouth.

"It must be love," the bartender thought, sadly. He was very close to being right.

MORE WACKY TAILS FROM
THE MISIDENTIFICATION EXPERT!
IN BOAT TRIP FROM HELL
SKUA!
THE BIRD IS LANDING IN THE WAKE!
WHERE'S THE SKUA FROM THAT FIRST WINTER HERRING GULL?
THE FIRST WINTER WHA, OH NO, THE SKUA MUSTA DROPPED OVER THE SWELL RIGHT BEHIND THE GULL!
WHAT A VIEW THOUGH!
LOOKED LIKE A FRESHLY MOLTED SECOND YEAR FEMALE IN ALTERNATE PLUMAGE!
I GOT FANTASTIC LOOKS AT THE OCHRACEOUS BUFF EDGES TO THE DISTAL PORTION OF THE MEDIAN UNDER PRIMARY COVERTS.
D'YALL SEE THAT?
THE LIGHTING WAS JUUUUST PUURRFECT!
FROM MY ANGLE, WITH MY SUPERB OPTICS, MY VIEW WAS JUUUUST RIGHT!
NICE!
TALK ABOUT SWEEEET!
OFCOURSE IVE SEEN THIS RACE ALLLLL OVER THE PLACE. IN FACT, I HELPED COAUTHOR A PAPER ON THE IDENTIFICATION OF THE BLAH, BLAH, BLAH, BLAH, BLAH
OH NO! THIS IS THE SAME JERK WHO WAS SCREAMING "YELLOW RAIL, YELLOW RAIL!" ON THE LAST BIRD-A-THON I WAS SEEN ON. I WAS AN IMMATURE THEN, BUT IT STILL BOTHERS ME!
STILL SORE HUH?
YOU BET I'M STILL SORA!
Keith Hansen 1993

Misidentification Expert

I have—and maybe you do, too—a wall full of books, mostly field guides. Field guides to every avian conglomerate conjured by science. First, second, and third editions of field guides to birds I don't have a prayer of seeing. Field guides to places that even Rand McNally hasn't heard of.

But among all these guides, there is not one that deals with one of birding's most common field problems: The Art of *Mis*-identification—the ability to blow an identification and then bamboozle your way clear.

Sure. Any person can misidentify a bird—and most people do. But blowing enough smoke to cover your boo-boo or convincing the gallery that you really saw a Cooper's Hawk (while everyone else was busy looking at the Sharp-shinned) takes real skill. It takes a misidentification expert.

How can you recognize a misidentification expert when you see one? That's easy. Misidentification experts have loud voices and in the midst of a group of novice birders they are invariably the first to shout out a bird name. Ah, but get a bunch of misidentification experts together, drop an immature jaeger in their midst, and all you'll hear is:

"Aha!"

"Ummmmm. Nice."

"Good One!"

"First one of *those* today."

Note: nobody actually identifies the bird. Why? Because they're experts. Experts don't have to identify birds. Experts already know what birds are. And if you never actually put a name to a bird, then you can never be proven wrong (which to a misidentification expert is much more important than ever being right).

So, the first trick in the art of misidentification is to establish yourself as an expert. You accomplish this by buying roof-prism binoculars, slapping Kenn Kaufman on the back in public, and writing long, rambling rebuttals to articles on the use of wing formulas to separate the races of *M. georgiana.*

Incidentally, this is another thing that distinguishes identification experts from misidentification experts. Identification experts initiate; misidentification experts castigate from the outside.

Here's another. Real experts make identification errors, because they are always trying to be better than they already are. Misidentification experts never make mistakes, because they are already better than anyone else could ever hope to be.

Misidentification experts are incredibly skilled at finding birds that sit on branches for about as long as the green flash sits on the horizon.

"Anyone *else* get a *good* look at that bird? No? Oh, too bad. *Beautiful* Lawrence's Warbler."

Misidentification experts are amazingly adept at finding birds flying at altitudes that are barely suborbital.

"Aaaaah . . . waaaay up thaaahr. No reference. Can't drop my binoculars or else . . . Ahhh . . . AH. Sorry. Disappeared in the haze. Peregrine for sure."

And misidentification experts are wonderfully skilled at identifying birds going dead away, into the sun, just below the horizon.

"Skua!"

But if the bird doubles back, a skilled misidentification expert will have "dropped the bird." If it lands in the chum slick and seems (at least to all the novices present) to be indistinguishable from a first winter Herring Gull, then it's not the bird the expert had.

In the event of an argument, skilled misidentification experts will have had a "better angle" than you did, can claim "*extensive* experience with the species," and will be able to draw upon esoteric, and hitherto unknown, field marks gleaned from the paper they are reviewing on "Tubenoses of the Ogalalla Aquifer" (or something like that). And . . .

"Incidentally, did you know that your new $1,300 binoculars have a serious chromatic aberration? Too bad."

Misidentification experts are not born. Becoming one is a long, hard process—in many ways, a more difficult process than just learning how to identify birds correctly in the first place.

Misidentification experts are also not terribly uncommon, so it astonishes me that no one has already written a field guide to the misidentification of North American birds. Just consider! There is only one correct identification for any species but almost an infinite number of misidentifications. Think of the possibilities. Think of all the sequels.

Come to think about it, I just might write the guide myself. Then wait for all the rebuttals to come in.

You Only Lose It Once

I knew, just *knew* that the grub-colored little reporter was going to ask *the* question before he opened his mouth. You could see it in the eyes. You could read the 54-point banner headline printed across his face:

BIRDERS EXPOSED AS PATHOLOGICAL LIARS. The subtitle read: "Records Committee Members Die in Mass Suicides."

Paralyzed by fatalism and horror I watched as the little vampire leaned forward and moved his lips, forming words.

"But how," the apparition whined, "do you know that birders are telling the truth?"

Pleased with the Pulitzer-worthy probe, the creature leaned back, savoring his moment of triumph.

If he had any guts, he'd have been a pornographer, I mused. "What?" I asked absently.

The face twisted in annoyance. "How do you know birders are telling the truth?" he repeated. "How do you know that birders don't just make all their sightings up?"

"Why would they want to do that?" I asked as earnestly as I knew how.

"I don't know," he crooned. "I'm just the reporter. Why don't *you* tell me?"

"But birders *don't* lie," I insisted. "It doesn't make sense for them to lie about the birds they see. Lying about the birds you see is like cheating at solitaire, like dating your sister."

Boo Radley's self-styled twin winked conspiratorially and

threw me a sideways glance. "Tell me," he coaxed. "I can keep your name out of this. I'll refer to you as an anonymous high-placed source. We'll set you up with a new identity and relocate you anyplace within our circulation radius. Tell me," he whispered.

The little reptile made me feel like I needed to take a bath.

I don't know why birding's underlying code of honesty is the source of so much skepticism, but it is and that's certainly a sad commentary on our times. Every time Christmas Bird Count season or the World Series of Birding rolls around, newspaper editors all over the country send out their cub reporters to "get the bird story." And every single one of them wants to know how *we know* that everyone sees what they said they saw.

For years, I just naively accepted birding's ethic of honesty on faith—accepted it because, well, let's face it, there are some truths that are just unassailable. You know: "*Cogito, ergo sum.*" "It ain't over till it's over." "Property is always your best investment." Things like that.

But after half a hundred reporters gnaw on the support struts of your faith, it begins to work on you. Trying to find a satisfactory response to an attack on *a priori* truth makes you reflective. And reflection opens the door to doubt. Pretty soon you find yourself wondering whether birders really are on the up and up about their sightings.

What if *you* were the only birder who was honest? Did you ever think of that? Boy, wouldn't that be a big joke on you.

And what makes you so certain that you've got Sir Galahad's blood running undiluted in your veins, anyway? What about that Curlew Sandpiper in that flock of Stilt Sandpipers that took off just when you arrived? Everyone in the crowd said the bird was in there. And you're pretty sure you got on the right one. Right?

Right?

So, with my faith shaken by a cynical press, I forced myself to reexamine one of birding's most fundamental principles. How can we be so certain that birders tell the truth?

Well, relax. If you crave reassurance, you'll be pleased to know that beneath birding's universal code there lies a practical prod. Birders don't cheat, because if they did, they'd get caught. Oh, sure, a person can get away with one or two spurious sightings. But the credibility of any birder who consistently finds birds that are out of the norm (a rash of inland jaegers sightings, Little Stints that can never be relocated) tarnishes amazingly fast. And credibility is like virginity. You only lose it once.

I stared back at the predatory little creature, trying to formulate a reply. One that would serve the truth and do justice to birding.

I wanted to tell him that only a reporter would ask such a stupid question and that I had never heard a birder raise the point. I wanted to tell him about deference and reciprocity, about mutual respect and trust that springs from shared interest—but sadly, I knew he wouldn't understand.

Most of all I wanted to explain how important credibility is and how jealously birders safeguard their reputations. But one look at him precluded that course, too.

Besides, he didn't want to hear any of this stuff. He wanted a scoop. He wanted a story.

So I gave him one.

"All right," I mumbled, "you got me. Birders lie through their teeth and I have evidence that members sitting on at least a dozen state rarities committees are on the take."

Nodding happily, he began to write.

"And we pull the wings off of butterflies. And we use our binoculars to roast ants on the sidewalk."

"Go on," he encouraged, "go on."

"All bird name changes are controlled by a secret cartel of field guide publishers called the Order of the Yellow Shaft[ed]. We barter our first-born male children for German optics. We sank the *Titanic.*"

"Oh, this is great," he shouted. "This is incredible!"

"We smuggle thousands of tons of cocaine into the country every spring, stashed in satchels that are strapped to the backs of Red Knots."

He filled the last page and began writing on his pants leg.

"Roger Tory Peterson is the Antichrist. The world will end when Bentam Basham records his nine hundredth North American life bird."

It was going to be one hell of a story. I hope he gets a Pulitzer.

The Secret Birding Journal of G. Washington of Virginia

A Note to the Reader

The package, string-tied and double-bag-wrapped, was stuffed in the mailbox. "Hope this isn't another road-killed bird needing identification," I thought to myself, wincing at the memory. The last one, deposited by a neighbor while I was on vacation, went a full ten count before anyone opened the box (and the postmistress hasn't forgiven me yet).

The package bore no return address; the postmark was dated March 30, from Baltimore, Maryland. It seemed too heavy for a T-shirt and too light for a bomb.

"Well, maybe a small bomb."

A rejected manuscript? No. The binoculars I sent off for realignment in 1967? No.

I hadn't entirely rejected the bomb idea—not that I specifically ordered one.

A little quick but delicate surgery disclosed a pile of moldy, bound parchment overrun with faded script. A typed Post-it note slapped over the title read: "Found in an old church in Baltimore. What do you think?" I pulled the note, held the top page closer to the light, and did my best to decipher the florid design.

If my collarbone hadn't gotten in the way, there is no telling where my jaw would have stopped. When I could see through the pain to read again I reached for the brittle pages and reread the impossible legend.

"The Collected Lifetime Observation of OUR OWN BIRDS *of*

the UNITED STATES *made by his* EXCELLENCY *G.* WASHINGTON *of Virginia as Compiled at his Request by his* LOVING *and* AGGRIEVED *wife, Martha."*

At the bottom of the page was a pen-and-ink drawing that looked like a pelican that had been tarred and feathered by Daniel Shay and burned by the British. The caption read: "The Great American Bald Eagle—MW."

"Whew," I thought. "I guess if I was responsible for a sketch that ugly I would have hidden the manuscript, too."

It took the better part of an evening to read it through. The manuscript itself is in poor condition, much of the text faded, some beyond recognition. As to its legitimacy, I'm no judge. It certainly has all the signs of great age upon it. I mean the paper isn't computer stock, typewriter bond, or even three-ring binder perforated (and you'd have to soak paper in a lot of pickle juice and bake it long enough to tenderize a scoter to get it to look the way this stuff does).

But as to whether or not G. Washington of Virginia—I mean, the *G. Washington of Virginia—was the author, well, that I couldn't say. Its legitimacy notwithstanding, the accounts are fascinating and if true, not only add a few chapters to the history of bird study in America but provide fascinating insight into the very roots of our republic.*

I leave it to readers to pass judgment as they may.

June 11, 1742

The cardinal red bird is a creature of uncommon attractiveness and boldness. It oft sits high atop some perch in plain open sight calling attention to itself by lusty singing. It seems strange to me that a bird so clad in a bright red coat would be so bold to stand in the open. It makes so easy a mark for the woodland hawks and marksmen.

Were I a bird, I would e'er be like the spot thrush of the woodland that is dressed in brown and much given to hide behind trees. I'faith it is hard to see and near impossible to shoot. I fain admire the cardinal red bird for its bold courage but think the bird stupid to wear so bright a red coat and stand so still and so long in open places.

July 4, 1745

'Tis unlikely that I will sit for a week. I'faith but my father is stern with his discipline and not one to stroke lightly with a switch. A hawke had nested in the branch of the cherry tree. I was ambitious to gather one or more of the young falcons and train them to hunt. 'Tis true they are small, but fearless and to fly one from the fist would be grand sport.

The tree was uncommonly difficult and my small hatchet ill suited for the task. But ere long the tree tottered and fell. I was hard put to reach even one hawk, still, and took many a bite for my trouble. Leaving I was surprised to espy a small gray owl sitting outside a hole opening to a different limb. It was dazed or confused by daylight (as owls are night birds) but flew as I reached for it. I marvel that two such hunting birds could live so close together yet govern their lives from separate branches.

September 2, 1749
Shenandoah Valley

While returning to our survey efforts, having rested during the heat of the day, I espied what seemed at first a leaf held by the web of a great black and yellow spider. Ere long I moved to investigate and, Marry! was surprised to find no leaf but a small woodland bird caught by a single feather of its wing. It hung suspended and could not break its bond.

What manner of bird it was I am helpless to say. In shape it was like unto the gray "yank" that walks on the trunks of trees but was smaller. It was vigorously striped black and white and its eye was pert and black.

I released it with no harm and admonished that henceforth it would do well to avoid such foreign entanglements.

May 1, 1777
Morristown, New Jersey

There is no turning back spring now. The oaks are in flower, horses grow fat, and the spirits of the men who suffered greatly this winter rise with the temperature. The roads will soon be dry enough for an army to move along. What will Howe do now I wonder?

I beheld a sight that was passing strange and sad. On the huts of the Pennsylvania line, a black-winged red bird, a bird I knew as a lad in Virginia, flew up and back again; landing first upon the roof of one hut, then another. Some of the men, because of its color, jested that it was a spy and would have shot it had not an officer interfered.

I recall it as a shy forest bird and I marvel to see it in so open a place. It seemed the bird was searching and confused and it comes to me that perhaps the bird was one that lived here and missed the trees cut last winter. It could not know that it perched on the very trees, now laid into huts. It remained all day, the only red coat in camp but seemed gone as evening settled.

June 15, 1782
Philadelphia, Pennsylvania

I suffer to think that having come so far the undoing of our struggle will be o'er a bird. What comes over Franklin that he should favor the turkey as a proper symbol for our fledgling nation? My regard for the bird, proper trussed and done to a turn, is surpassed by no man—not even Franklin whose love of victuals surpasses legend. But to elevate a common table fowl to the stature of the National Bird goes beyond reason.

I have no trifle with the eagle, as some have favored, though it feeds upon carrion and seems at the mercy of crows. For my part, I favor the Great Ivory-beaked Woodpecker—a noble bird whose colors recall somewhat our flag. It is industrious and fearless and much prized by the savage. It lives in the deep forests that stretch in limitless fashion so will never know shortage. Its hammering is like the ax falls of the woodsman and its golden eye hath an intelligence that the turkey lacks.

What is more, 'tis unlikely that any man would deign eat the bird unless faced by starvation whereas turkey is common on the table. It doth not show proper respect, I think, to carve and serve the national symbol. As well we might have to eat our own words after fighting long in order to be able to openly speak them.

December 13, 1799
Mt. Vernon

I am taken to bed with fever so have opportunity to write of the bird I chanced upon while riding. If not new to this region it was at least one I have not seen in a long life. A great flock of blackbirds was feeding amid the field animals. One among them caught my eye as it seemed to have a golden head. I could not shoot for fear of hitting one of the animals and each time I approached the flock took wing.

The golden-headed blackbird seemed larger with white on the wing where many of the marsh blackbirds have red. But the wariness of the birds defeated me. I could not approach to a distance that would permit study or safe release of shot.

It occurs to me that a spyglass would have aided me greatly in my effort. My eyes get no better with the years and my skill with a fowling piece is not as it was. Though I have not admitted it to any but myself, I find, too, I relish less and less the hunt. Perhaps the spyglass is the answer. It will satisfy the curiosity and lessen the bloodletting. When this magnificent cough subsides, I will write to Jefferson about this. He has a quick mind for contrivances, though Franklin, near ten years in his grave, had a genius for spectacles.

I feel certain the bird is not native here, for I have not seen it before. There are, I doubt not, many new wonders to be found on this great continent. This next century will be one filled with discovery. I look forward to it, God willing.

Birder of Fortune

The sky opened up clearing the street—something the New York City Vice Squad had been unable to do in its long, illustrious history. I aimed for an innocuous-looking storefront sandwiched between something called "Massage Plus" and another enterprise touting "Madam Limbo—Mystic Reader." I would have aimed for Madam Limbo's but I already knew my fortune. I was going to miss my bus.

A hand-printed sign taped to the door caught my eye: BIRDER OF FORTUNE OUTFITTERS.

"Odd," I thought. "Never heard of them." Curiosity and trepidation played tug-of-war with my resolve. Curiosity won a close decision and I edged into the room.

The place looked like an I.R.A. stronghold and smelled like the inside of Alexander Wilson's boot. The most impressive feature was a leering, larger-than-life-sized poster of Chuck Norris. He was dressed like a full armored division and photographed in the act of ripping a National Geographic Society's *Field Guide to North American Birds* in two. The poster read: FIE ON FIELD MARKS! KILL THEM ALL AND LET PROTEIN ELECTROPHORESIS SORT IT OUT.

"We have it in wallet size, too," someone offered my left ear—and if words can slither then these slithered.

I turned to find myself nose to nose with a short, shabby figure that looked as if he'd been fed to moths. He smiled, filling the air with the scent of tuna on rye.

"You must be Tex," he observed, nodding. "Our, uh, 'mutual

friend' described you perfectly. You're going to be very happy with this year's bird. Another North American first," he added.

"What?" I whispered.

"Oh, dear," the proprietor said. "Aren't you the gentleman from the Greater Rio Grande Valley Chamber of Commerce?"

I shook my head.

"My mistake," he said, studying me closely. "Are you a new customer? Can I help you with something special?"

"No. Thank you," I said, smiling, measuring the distance to the door. "Just looking."

He spread his arms in a gesture of welcome. "Don't look! Find. Only tyros look."

I wandered over to a pile of Peterson *Field Guides,* 5th edition.

"Odd," I thought, "I didn't know Roger had completed another revision." Each guide bore an inscription in red ink that read: "Thanks for the Life Bird," signed "Rog."

"You can have them personalized," the "prop" shouted.

I nodded slowly. "I think he prefers 'Roger.'"

The prop looked unhappy. "Well, 'Rog' sounds so much more chummy, don't you think?" Then he brightened. "But for a little extra we can customize one for you."

Past a special bird "banding" section featuring Italian designer mist nets, three grades of tanglefoot (custom-blended for your climate and region), and Stinger rocket net launchers was a wall offering a global assortment of prechecked checklists; 600, 700, and 800 Club membership certificates; and ghostwritten rare-bird report forms, cross-catalogued by location and species. Just fill in your name and the date. Documenting photos ten dollars extra; specimens arranged by request.

"They're guaranteed," the prop shouted. "The report passes your State Bird Records Committee or your money is fully refunded."

In the back of the shop was a target range. On a table, displayed beneath a sign that read "Put birding's future in your hands today!" were a bulky pair of binoculars and an opened box of screw-on filters.

I selected the one marked "Waterfowl," turned the instrument on an assortment of stuffed birds down range, and peered into the binoculars. The edge of the field, I discovered, was filled with stenciled, labeled duck silhouettes. To make an identification, all you had to do was match the mounted bird down range with the silhouette in the glass. Pretty clever, actually.

"Try the squelch button," a tuna-tainted voice pleaded. "That's the best part."

I superimposed a silhouette marked "Smew" over a stuffed Gadwall, pushed "squelch," and watched, horrified, as the image of a male Gadwall was trimmed to fit the Smew contours. I tried it on Muskovy, Whooper Swan, and Labrador Duck silhouettes with the same results.

"But with this thing, you can make any bird look like anything you want!" I protested.

"That's right," the prop agreed. "That's why it's so expensive."

I felt a hand on my elbow and was almost brought to my knees by the smell of rancid tuna. "Listen, why don't you and I step around back? That's where we keep the stuff we reserve for our very special customers."

I broke free and started for the door, backing directly into the paunch of a prosperous-looking gentleman wearing a Stetson and a car salesman's grin.

"Howdy," he drawled. "I'm here to pick up that Happy Eagle critter we ordered."

"Harpy Eagle," I corrected. "Talk to that man right there," I said pointing. And then I *ran*—all the way to the Port Authority bus terminal (making one short stop en route). Clay Sutton, coauthor of *Hawks in Flight,* and I have a standing wager regarding the identity of the next raptor species to occur in North America. I wanted to change my bet.

Keith Hansen 1993

Ten!

In June, when sunlight dominates the Northern Hemisphere, road-weary birders can play highway games to stay alert and keep boredom at bay.

"Yellow-headed Blackbird on the right! Trip bird."

Or *" 'Nuther Red-tailed Hawk on the fencepost. That makes thirty-four."* But in December, when darkness commands, highway diversions are few and quickly spent. And we'd listened to every cassette in our collection a dozen times, wife Linda and I. We'd played out every conceivable conversation at least twice and argued every pressing socioeconomic issue to the point of blind indifference.

And I-10 across Texas seems to run on forever—at least the span of a human life—but probably forever.

And there might have been a thousand miles behind us, but there were still two thousand miles to go.

I realized, suddenly, that Linda's face was turned my way and that a question must have been asked.

"What?" I said, to prove I'd been listening.

"I said, what are your ten favorite birds?"

"Oh," I said, momentarily taken aback. "I guess I'd have to think about it."

"Take your time," she offered. "We're two days from home."

I did think about it. In fact, I found myself getting positively intrigued by the question. Think about it yourself. All the birds on the planet. All the color, song, plumages, adaptations, finesse, and skills. Add to these compelling attributes the human bonding factor, the irreplaceable memories that mark the encounters of your birding lifetime. *Now* try to pare a list of favorites down to . . .

"Only ten?" I asked.

"Only ten," Linda affirmed.

"How about an even dozen," I pleaded.

"Ten," Linda insisted. "Or put it this way. If you were shipwrecked on some uncharted island and had to spend the rest of your life there, what ten birds would you choose to keep you company?"

"That's easy," I said. "Turkey, chicken, goose, game hen, pheasant . . ."

"Be serious," she chastised.

"I am serious," I insisted.

"Assume we'll have an unlimited supply of food."

"Oh, you're on this island, too."

"Of course I'm on the island. I'm your wife."

"Then we've got to have consensus with this list."

"Sure," Linda said. "Unless you want to spend the rest of your life on a desert island with a very disgruntled birding wife."

It wasn't an attractive prospect.

"OK," I replied. "Who chooses first?"

"You do," she said magnanimously and I confess I grabbed the opportunity before she had a chance to change her mind.

"Swallow-tailed kite!" I shouted, putting a name to my absolute all-time favorite bird. If the divine creator had set out to cast a dream in feathers, S/He couldn't have managed any better.

"Merlin," Linda countered.

"We can't have two raptors," I objected.

"Why not?" Linda demanded.

"Because we only have ten slots to fill," I pointed out.

"So?" Linda said.

"So there are still some 170 families and about 9,000 possibilities floating around in the world."

"Let's limit the scope to North American birds," she offered.

"That still leaves us nearly one hundred possibilities for every slot," I explained, confident that the weight of this disclosure would be sufficient for a spouse (even *my* most stubborn of all spouses) to see the error of her ways and recall her candidate.

"Your turn," she observed.

"You're not going to pick something else?" I demanded.

"Merlin's my favorite bird," she said, smiling.

There is no contesting such an irrefutable point, and after all this *was* the woman I was going to spend the rest of my life on an island with. Besides, I had to admit I like Merlins, too. The feistiest, most pugnacious little beastie ever set on wings. A bird that can fly rings around a Peregrine and make chutney out of the most acrobatic swallow at whim or need.

"All right," I said, relenting. "But make it a Blue Jack."

"A Richardson's Blue Jack," Linda promised, naming the powder blue subspecies that shines like an oiled sword blade. "Done," I said. "Hmmm," I mused. "*An island.* We're going to need a seabird or two, don't you think?"

"Like a shearwater?" Linda suggested after a moment's thought.

"Like a shearwater," I agreed, mentally running through the ranks of birds whose flight makes the poetry of Tennyson seem pinioned and earthbound.

"How about Buller's?" I said, selfishly putting a name to a species I had seen in both the Pacific *and* the Atlantic oceans. Every time I see the species off Monterey, I recall that day off New Jersey and the silver-winged heartstopper of a bird that showed up in a flock of Greater Shearwaters for an Atlantic Coast record.

"OK," Linda said. "Buller's. How about waterfowl?"

"Wood Duck," I suggested.

"Too gaudy," Linda assessed.

"Hooded Merganser," I offered.

"Oldsquaw!" she asserted. A great choice, I had to admit. "Owls?" she invited.

"Not so fast!" I objected. "What about gulls and terns?"

"We've already got a shearwater," she offered.

"We've already got a pair of raptors, too," I pointed out.

"You're NOT going to HAVE an OWL?" Linda exclaimed. Both her intonations and her expression suggested that I'd just confessed that I'd never taken a bath. But she had a point. What would the rest of your life be without an owl?

"OK, OK," I soothed. "Take it easy. How about Ross' Gull *and* Snowy Owl?"

There was silence while Linda considered these options.

"You know," she said, "if you're going to spend the rest of your life on an island, you might want to make it a *tropical* island instead of one stuck in the Bering Strait."

"It's an imaginary island," I defended, "therefore magical. There's no problem having Snowy Owls and swallow-tailed kites on a magical island."

"Why Ross' Gull?" she demanded.

"It's a functional hybrid between a Little Gull and a Roseate Tern—two great birds for the price of one."

Linda nodded. "Why Snowy Owl?"

"To keep you from saying Ferruginous Pygmy-Owl and getting a life bird up on me," I admitted, smiling.

Linda grimaced and shook her head (but what she thought of the duplicitous nature of husbands she kept to herself).

"You know," she observed, "it's getting to be an awful quiet island. And Snowy Owls aren't the most musical of critters."

There was no contesting this observation. Of the birds that had secured a place in our lineup, none—with the possible exception of Oldsquaws—are accounted among the earth's great vocalists.

"Oldsquaws sound kind of neat," I offered.

"If you like the sound of fox hounds gargling."

"What are you saying?" I asked. "That you don't want Oldsquaw, now?"

"No. I'm saying I want a screech owl."

"*Screech owl,*" I mused. Sure. Why not? I thought back to all the whistled duets on Christmas Bird Counts and Big Days. I thought of all the nights at home that my dreams had been shaken by a whinny and of wooded western canyons flooded with starlight and the musical toots of owls.

"Eastern, Western, or Whiskered?" I asked.

"Western," said my western wife.

"How many does that make so far?" I demanded.

"Six," she said.

"SIX!" I exclaimed. "Why, we haven't even hit passerines yet."

"And we skipped shorebirds—not to mention herons and egrets."

"NO SHOREBIRDS!" I screeched—taking Linda's cue and not mentioning herons and egrets, either. (You've got to cut corners somewhere.) "We've got to have a shorebird."

"Try and pick something more colorful than a mud flat," Linda pleaded.

"Sure," I promised, "sure." "*Phalaropes . . . Curlew Sandpiper . . . Hudsonian Godwit,*" I thought, picking through the possibilities like a Sanderling moving down the tide line. "*Red Knot . . . Ruddy Turnstone . . . Whimbrel . . .*" There were just too many to choose from. Too much animation, too many handsome plu—

"Plover!" I exclaimed.

"Can you be a bit more vague?" Linda chided.

"I want a plover," I asserted. "It would go perfectly with the beach. And give your Merlin something to chase," I added.

"So you want a Semipalmated-sized plover?" Linda assessed.

Actually, I didn't. I wanted a full-sized plover—either a Lesser Golden- or a Black-bellied. And I wanted the Merlin to harass the bird, not eat it (not that a Merlin can't manage a magnum-sized plover if it has a mind to).

I was leaning toward golden, wondering whether to go with one of the racy *fulvas* or stick to the domestic *dominica,* until the whistle of a Black-bellied Plover surfaced in my mind—surely one of the most haunting calls in nature.

"Black-bellied," I said. "In high plumage."

Linda nodded. "Need a hummingbird," she observed.

Of *course* we needed a hummingbird. What would life on a magical island be without the earth's most magical bird? But which hummingbird?

"Your call," I said, punting the dilemma away.

Linda put on a ponder. She looked at her reflection in the

glass. She looked at her hands in her lap. Finally she looked at me.

"Anna's," she said, surprising me.

"Why Anna's?" I asked. "I'd have bet you'd say Magnificent."

"Anna's reminds me of home," she said—and whether she was thinking of her childhood in California or her mother, Anne, she wouldn't say.

"Then I want a Blue Jay," I announced loudly.

"WHAT?" Linda said, even more loudly.

"Blue Jays remind *me* of home," I said, and they do—recall the eastern woodlands where I grew up.

"That makes nine then," Linda observed.

"Oh!" I said, and my mind leaped ahead to all the birds that hadn't been considered, all the birds that would be missed. "I guess I'd rather have a thrush than a Blue Jay." It would be hard to live in a world in which thrushes didn't sing.

"Varied," my western wife suggested.

"Wood," her parochial-minded husband insisted.

"Hermit?" Linda pleaded.

"Wood," I said.

"Then I get to choose the warbler," Linda said, "and I choose Painted Redstart."

A terrific choice! A wonderful choice. The Arizona specialty might not take top honors in the vocalization category, but in color and animation the bird scores a perfect "10" all by itself. As a matter of sad fact, it was ten—number ten. Our list was complete.

"But we don't have an oriole or tanager or bunting," I pleaded.

"Or a wren, or a sparrow," Linda added.

"We'll live out the rest of our lives without ever seeing another crossbill or a kingfisher."

"Or a ptarmigan. Or a jaeger."

Linda and I turned as one and said as one: "No *jaeger!*" No Long-tailed Jaeger. "The sexiest bird that flies," in the estimate and words of the late pelagic mavin, Tom Davis. It was unthinkable. It was . . .

"Time to rethink this list," Linda said, and we did. Added

Long-tailed Jaeger and dumped the shearwater and Ross' Gull. We figured Long-tailed Jaeger embodied many of the attributes of both. That gave us one last slot to fill.

"We need a sparrow," Linda observed. "There's got to be something coming to the feeder."

We certainly did need a sparrow. One sparrow. One favored species drawn from those subtle, secretive ranks that birders discover late in their development and come to love.

I thought of Henslow's—my last North American lifer. I considered the chestnut-napped LeConte's, the silver-voiced Vesper, the dandified Lark Sparrow, the dapper Black-throated, and the gentrified White-crowned. I thought of Aleutian Song Sparrows and the challenge of Five-stripeds and the musical twittering of American Tree Sparrows that has brightened more winter days than I can count or recall.

I thought of taking the easy way out and picking a Pyrrhuloxia or a longspur instead, and then I thought of something else.

"What about Fox Sparrow?" I invited. It's a great looker and the song is rich, almost comical.

Linda considered each of these points but I could see that she wasn't entirely won over.

"There's one more consideration. If we take Fox Sparrow, we might consider passing on Wood Thrush. One island isn't big enough for two big spot-breasted birds. And if we dump the thrush, we'll still have one slot open."

Linda nodded. "Then I get to choose the last bird," she said. It wasn't a question. "You chose first; I choose last." It was incontestably proper and fair.

"OK," I said reluctantly. "Make it a good one."

"House Sparrow," she announced.

"*HOUSE SPARROW*!" I exploded.

"House Sparrow," she affirmed.

"WHAT ON EARTH FOR?" I demanded.

"Got to have something for my Merlin to eat," she explained. "Or do you want to sacrifice your plover?"

"Oh, yeah," I said.

That People Should Be Happy

I nosed my car into the parking area and claimed a random spot. I could have had just about any space, anywhere. There was only one other car in a lot designed for twenty.

Despite the clinging fog that promised wet times ahead, there was no accounting for such fortune. South Cape May, New Jersey, is one of the hottest birding spots on the circuit, and this was peak season. My friend Patty and I would have the place to ourselves, it seemed, and I began to anticipate a pleasant morning of easy birding and catching up on two geographically estranged lives.

It was at this moment of vulnerability that the occupant of the other car pounced.

"Hello, fellow sufferer," he hailed, as he closed the short distance between us. His course, I noted, cut a little bit inside, precluding any hope of escape toward my car (a professional touch I couldn't help but admire). Clearly, this was a man who was used to boring people, one skillfully adept at pinning down strangers in conversation.

Vainly, I searched the road for Patty's car, sighed, and surrendered to my fate.

He was a short man, an energetic man, the sort of person who dabbles in everything and has never voiced a contradiction he couldn't ignore. His accent said Brooklyn, the plates on his sedan, Florida. I figured him for a retired barber or vacuum-cleaner salesman, with dentist an outside possibility.

I guessed he was a widower. I *knew,* beyond question or doubt, that he was very, very lonely.

"Nothing much out there," he proclaimed marking the borders of "out there" with a sweep of his hand that covered about 280 degrees. "I've been around once already. We've got our work cut out for us, that's for sure."

The suggestion of plurality did not escape me.

The observations of my new friend notwithstanding, from the parking lot, at least, there seemed to be a great deal of activity "out there."

The moisture-laden air carried a cacophony of shorebird noises: the *"crips"* and *"creeps"* and *"jeets"* of assorted sandpipers. The tumble of notes that are a dowitcher's song. The haunting whistle of a Black-bellied Plover and the ringing cry of a Greater Yellowlegs.

Frankly, the meadows had never sounded busier.

Not wishing to hurt the fellow's feelings with a direct contradiction, I decided to cushion my rebuff with a temporal modifier.

"Yesterday," I began . . .

"Yesterday," he agreed, "I saw some herons, egrets, and Great Black-headed Gulls."

"Laughing Gulls?" I suggested. There are Great Black-backed Gulls (which are very common in Cape May), and Black-headed Gulls, which superficially resemble Laughing Gulls (but are very uncommon in Cape May).

There even is a *Larus* species named "Great Black-headed Gull," but to the best of my knowledge this mostly Asian species has never been recorded in the Western Hemisphere. On this basis, I judged that the chances of the fellow's having seen one (much less several) to be slim. Laughing Gulls, in Cape May, on the other hand, are as regular as soup cans on a grocer's shelf.

The fellow was not to be dissuaded.

"No, Great Black-headed Gulls," he insisted. "Here," he said, searching at random through the pages of a battered field guide. "Black-headed Gull," he said, triumphantly pointing to an illustration on one of the pages, untroubled, it seemed, by the caption that read: "Laughing Gull."

Following this success, the fellow decided to capitalize on his advantage by producing a trump.

"But today," he proclaimed, relishing the disclosure, "I found one of those little sandpipers with the band across the chest. The . . . uh . . . uh . . ."

"Semipalmated Plover?" I coached.

"Semi-*pal*-mated Plover," he corrected. "I haven't seen one of those since I used to lead nature walks for [he named a scout troop]. They're rare, you know."

Actually, they are not rare. In the Arctic, where they breed, they are quite common. In May, along the Atlantic Coast, they are ubiquitous. In the South Cape May Meadows, during the last week or so, they'd been all over the place.

There must have been something about my silence that he read as skepticism, something in my expression that galvanized him to action.

"Come on," he said, shouldering the burden of leadership. "I'll see if I can find it for you again."

I hesitated and came very close to telling him the truth: that I had seen *thousands* of Semipalmated Plovers; that they *weren't* at all uncommon; and that, in fact, four were dropping into the Meadows at that very moment.

But as harsh as these truths might be, they were mere shadows of the more fundamental honesty, which was that I had precious little time to go birding these days, that I wasn't eager for his company, and that I had better things to do than amuse the likes of him.

Ten years ago, I might have been this honest and this blunt, but that was before a pivotal conversation with the proprietors of a hotel in Cape May. A conversation that added breadth to life.

There was an argument. It had something to do with a block of rooms that was supposed to be put aside (and wasn't), or put aside and summarily canceled (and wasn't). It doesn't matter now. It hardly mattered then. But both the proprietor and I were pretty heated up about the whole thing and in the middle of the argument, the proprietor's husband walked in, a gentle man whose eyes looked like an apology.

He stood with his back to us for a time, listening but not intruding. Then he turned and said, "Sarah, what's the problem?"

Sarah went into a caustic diatribe that reflected poorly (and probably not inaccurately) upon me. But before her climbing irritation could reach its peak, her husband reached out with a frail hand and touched her lightly on her bare arm.

"Sarah," he admonished, gently, "that people should be happy. *That* is the important thing."

Tattooed on the man's wrist was the ghoulish number that branded him a Nazi concentration camp survivor.

That, I recall thinking at the time, *is a tough school to graduate from.* And if one of the tenets of this man's life is that other people's happiness is important, then I would be wise to accept this doctrine as my own.

And so I have. Or, at least, I have tried.

"It won't take much time," my newfound friend encouraged. "I know right where it was."

"All right," I said, relenting. "Just let me get my spotting scope."

We walked down the center road. He led, I followed. Along the way, I learned that Skippy peanut butter doesn't stick to the roof of your mouth like store-brand varieties; that wool insulates better than cotton when it's wet; that if I invested in bonds I'd be making a higher return than keeping my money tied up in a regular interest-bearing account; and that Alabama has the finest highway rest stop facilities in the country.

The fog began to lift as we hit the flats. Several hundred shorebirds were feeding in the grassy pools—assorted sand-pipers, dowitchers, two species of phalaropes, and a couple dozen Semipalmated Plovers.

My friend began searching the flocks with his binoculars—panning through the birds, using all his skill and superhuman determination to relocate the bird he'd promised me. And I wish that fortune had been kinder, had allowed him to find a plover and show it to me. It would have made him happy and it probably would have made a better story. But it wasn't to be.

Patty had arrived and was approaching at a brisk walk. Not understanding the situation, it seemed certain that she would betray my unconfided skills—embarrassing us both. I put my scope on a distant group of shorebirds and asked the fellow's council about "the bird all the way to the left."

He *knew* he could find it for me.

"What was that all about?" Patty asked later.

I tried to explain.

"He wanted to show *you* a Semipalmated Plover?" she demanded.

I nodded.

"But they're not even uncommon!" she observed, plainly perplexed.

I nodded again.

"Why did you do it?" she asked.

"That people should be happy," I chanted. "That's the important thing."

"You're such a jerk," she said. "Come on. Let's go birding."

I nodded again, smiled, saying nothing. There seemed no reason to contradict her.

The Art of Pishing

I'm a pisher. Some birders are; some aren't. Me? I pish. Couldn't bird without it.

"Pishing" is an onomatopoeic term applied to the orally produced noises made by bird watchers to lure songbirds out of cover. If this is not the definition that you had in mind then you were confusing pishing with something else.

There are pishers and there are pishers. Some practitioners are fairly low key in their approach. They will step in front of a likely looking hedge, utter a timorous "psssst" or whispered "shhhhhhh," and wait. If vireo X or warbler Y doesn't appear in timely fashion they slink away.

Most patrons of the art are more tenacious. Some will wheeze or shush themselves into unconsciousness before admitting that a hedge is empty of aviformes. Often one pisher in full chorus will attract other pishers. It's not uncommon to see half a dozen pishers in full song all standing around a bush, sounding like an assortment of perforated steam pipes.

Why, you ask, would a bird go out of its way to investigate a leaky steam pipe? Because pishing is thought to mimic the generic scolding calls used by assorted passerines. The theory goes like this. If a bird becomes pish piqued, it will go out of its way to investigate the situation, and add its own voice to the ruckus. This in turn will attract more pish-piqued birds. Who will, in turn, join the harangue. Which will in turn attract more birds. Who will in turn . . .

But does it work?

I posed this question to the late Dr. Harold Axtell, a former museum curator who was to birding what Hammurabi was to law. Harold had made an exhaustive study of pishing (along with every other facet of birding) and concluded that, depending upon circumstance, pishing will do one of three things. It will (*a*) attract birds, (*b*) scare birds away, or (*c*) do nothing.

Why would a birder bother with a technique that offers less than a coin-toss chance of success?

Some do it for the sense of mastery it gives them. Some do it out of sloth because, let's face it, if the bird can't be coaxed to you, you've got to go to it.

Most do it because when pishing works, it works very well. Chris Abrams, a British friend, became a pishing adept during a trip to the U.S. The British have never practiced the art because pishing elicits about as much response from your average Old World birds as it does from your average Stonehenge pillar.

Anyway, one day Chris joined a troop of British birders that was wrapped sixty deep around a hedge in which a "Yank Warbler," a Northern Parula, was alleged to be hiding. The silence was so profound some professed to be able to hear the bird's heartbeat.

Chris waited along with the rest for what he deemed was a decent interval. Then, without warning, he cut loose with a noise which some likened to an enraged ninety-pound Siamese with a lisp, others to a steam engine in the grips of a grand mal seizure. Half those present rushed to save a comrade whom they assumed was dying. The other half rushed to kill him.

Luckily for Chris, the warbler popped to the top of the bush and sat until everyone got bored (which for British birders is a long time).

This brings up another interesting point. Pishing entices some species out of bushes better than others. Most warblers, chickadees, and titmice respond nicely. Sparrows, on the other hand, dig little burrows at the first little "psst." Sedge Wrens put their alulae in their mouths and sulk. And trying to entice a Connecticut Warbler to venture out of its poison ivy stronghold is tantamount to pishing into the wind.

Occasionally, pishing works *too* well. While leading a workshop group in Cape May one morning I stepped in front of a likely-looking bayberry thicket and broke into my best imitation of an apoplectic titmouse. Almost immediately a bleary-eyed Yellow-rumped Warbler burst to the top of a bush and in .000367 seconds went from 0 to 60 mph in the company of a very surprised (but not displeased) Merlin.

Birders will argue tirelessly over the merits of pishing. Why it works for some species and not others. Why it works sometimes and not other times. Whether pishing does or does not place undue stress on birds. Whether it causes sterility, birth defects, or brain damage.

One overlooked consideration, a point in pishing's favor, is probably worth noting. Even if all the strange, rude, and embarrassing noises that constitute pishing have no effect whatsoever on birds, pishing is still a fair substitute for patience. It forces a body to stand in place for an extended period of time. And, over much of the world, if you stand in one place long enough, a bird is bound to appear.

Keith Hansen
1993

Little Lost Blue

"Stop," Pete commanded, and there's a lot of command wrapped up in the likes of my ol' friend Pete Bacinski. I was amenable to suggestion (as amenable as people who have gone thirty-one straight hours without sleep can be) and Saab 9000s are obliging little beasts.

But there are certain laws governing bodies in motion. And how they tend to stay in motion. So it took a little time for Pete's will to be reflected in a *complete* stop (not that anyone actually waited that long). No time to dawdle on a Big Day—a twenty-four-hour test of birding skills in which each species found counts as one.

Before the anguished screech of tires had faded, four doors were in motion. Before the key was out of the ignition, the other members of the Zeiss Guerrilla Birding Team had stepped onto the roadway—into a spring morning that smelled like the Michelin man had backed into a Bunsen burner.

Bacinski led the charge. This was his turf and his stakeout. *Pete Bacinski,* coordinator of the Highland's breeding-bird survey. *Pete Bacinski,* who is on a first-name basis with every nesting warbler in the tract (and who knew their parents and grandparents, too). *Pete Bacinski,* who can tell you that the only surefire place to find a Black-throated Blue Warbler on a workable New Jersey Big Day route is . . .

"Here," he whispered, gesturing toward a wall of second-growth woodlands. "I had the female yesterday. Just wait."

We did wait, patient as sprinters in the blocks. *Watching* for a vibrating branch. *Listening* for a telltale "chip" or a diagnostic song. Waited five . . . ten . . . fifteen . . . almost *thirty seconds!*

Almost an eternity on a Big Day.

"Come on, bird," Pete pleaded in tones one usually reserves for the bumper ahead of you in a New Jersey Turnpike traffic jam.

"*Shpeee, shpee, shpee, shpee, shpee, shpeesh,*" he urged, translating his plea into "Pish," a universal bird language that is to passerines what Swahili is to East African tribes.

But the bird didn't speak Pish. We tried "Squeek" and "Chip" in sundry dialects and finally "Whinny" (an ancient hunting language spoken by screech owls) with much the same results. None of us spoke Esperanto and tapes, of course, are banned from the World Series of Birding.

After two minutes or so, teammate Don Freiday's attention had wandered toward the clouds and any raptors that might be passing by. Rick Radis, too, had accepted the inevitable. Wife Linda glanced at her watch.

"The bird was right here *yesterday,*" Pete promised, stung by the treachery of the bird's betrayal. "It came right out."

"Fie on 'em," I pronounced. (Well, something like that, anyway.) "We'll just have to dig out a migrant somewhere along the route."

Pete's expression said he didn't believe me and I can't fault him for that. I didn't believe it either.

We sprinted to the car and four doors slammed with a report like a graveside salute. The Saab growled to life and before the growl could soften to a purr a kicked-down accelerator brought the turbo to a scream. There was still four hundred miles of Big Day route ahead and precious little time for looking behind. We'd have a whole year to wallow in that kind of contemplation. Starting tomorrow.

I won't say I understand the allure of Big Days, understand what it is that prompts otherwise well-adjusted adults to behave like pool balls after a break, run around like lobotomized hamsters, and ring up birds with the aesthetic appreciation of an electronic price scanner. A Big Day brings out the Jekyll and Hyde in us and maybe a little Don Quixote and Karl von Clausewitz, too. It combines the truant allure of an all-night poker game and the camaraderie of the ol' deer camp.

Once each year, old men play it and say to themselves, "See, I can still keep up with those young pups. Why, with just a little exercise I'm sure . . ."

Once each year, younger men do it and reach for the stars set beyond the reach of mortals by the immortal elders. A Big Day is a stone skipped across a lake for no other reason except last year you got nine splashes and this year you want ten. It's a ritual, a rite of spring that binds us to birding's past and offers communion with the elders whose passion for Big Days may even have surpassed our own.

The roots of Big Day reach deep into birding's origins and the tendrils extend all across the country. But the early hotbed of Big Day interest was unquestionably the Northeast; the two men most responsible for stoking the coals were Ludlow Griscolm of Massachusetts and Charles Urner of New Jersey. Both men were Big Day fanatics, and they often teamed up to conduct their Big Day runs.

On May 19, 1927, the two set out to beat back a challenge issued by Allan Cruickshank and R. J. Kuerzi, who had recorded 120 species in the "Bronx region" on May 15—a new record for the Atlantic Coast. Griscolm and Urner began their quest in Troy Meadows, a large freshwater marsh thirty miles west of Manhattan. Morning found them working the hills around Boonton for migrants, then on to Essex County Reservation, and finally to the Elizabeth and Newark estuaries. Their strategy and skill garnered 130 species and the new record.

Big Day routes are not stagnant. Like rock gardens and outboard motors, they require constant fiddling and periodic overhaul. Urner's route was no exception. It got longer and the ante got higher. In 1928 Urner's appetite for a bigger list carried him as far south as coastal Manasquan, New Jersey. This necessitated three extra hours of drive time but it garnered a whopping 145 species. One year later the route was extended to Brigantine, near Atlantic City, an unheard-of distance in those days of two-lane roadways.

I can picture them, these greats of the founding age, sitting around Urner's kitchen table in the dark hour before dawn, making last-minute adjustments to their carefully crafted route. I can see the string of dark figures mincing their way down secret trails through Troy Meadows, their pants soaked by morning dew, their breath leaving puffs of vapor where they pass. I can envision the line faltering as one of the leaders stops . . . cups hands behind ears . . . then gestures into the darkness.

You can name the birds seen by these Urner Club members because they are matters of record. Between 1930 and 1950 American Bittern was tallied twenty out of twenty years; Least Bittern nineteen out of twenty; Virginia Rail, twenty out of twenty; Sora, twenty out of twenty.

Have I imagined it or have I really seen faded photos of men perched on running boards driving slowly down back roads, ears cocked and eyes alert for the birds of spring? Birds like: Red-shouldered Hawk (20/20), Upland Plover (19/20), Brown Thrasher (20/20), Least Flycatcher (20/20), Worm-eating Warbler (20/20), Chestnut-sided Warbler (20/20), Parula Warbler (20/20), Black-throated Blue Warbler (20/20), Myrtle Warbler (20/20), Black-throated Green Warbler (19/20), Blackpoll Warbler (20/20), Hooded Warbler (20/20), Canada Warbler (20/20), Magnolia Warbler (19/20), Olive-backed Thrush (20/20), Gray-cheeked Thrush (20/20), Henslow's Sparrow (19/20), Vesper Sparrow (19/20).

I know I have seen, in a dog-eared scrapbook, candid shots of Big Day birders up to their tired, bare asses in the surf off the southern tip of Long Beach Island. I can only take my hat off to men who, at the end of a Big Day, would contemplate that murderous march through sand (or would jump into fifty-degree ocean water).

Urner's predicted 160 was forged into reality in 1930, but the high-water mark wasn't reached until 1933. On May 14, 1933, Urner, Ludlow Griscolm, Joe Hickey, Richard Pough, and the rest of an *eleven-person hit squad,* ran Urner's fine-tuned route and nailed 173 species for the party list (including Yellow Rail and Arctic Tern!). It was a record that lasted a long, long time.

The Saab bounced down a road that barely rates inclusion on a New Jersey road map. "There's one other place that *might* have a Black-throated Blue," Pete counseled. "I think it's worth a try."

We tried it. And it didn't.

We drove right past the "Hills of Boonton," Urner's dawn site, but never gave a thought to stopping there. Nobody's run a Big Day route through that sterile suburban patchwork in years.

We could have gambled and gone down to New Jersey Audubon's Scherman-Hoffman Sanctuaries or the Great Swamp National Wildlife Refuge, but that would have added a half hour to our route with no promise of tangible return—not a very smart thing to do on a Big Day.

No, one way or another, we were committed to our strategy, the same strategy now used by most teams entered in the annual World Series of Birding Big Day competition—a strategy that is, like Urner's, predicated upon the times.

Their strategy hinged upon catching the waves of migrating birds that sweep across the Northeast during May. *Today's* strategy calls for a methodical, point-by-point, bird-by-bird inventory of staked-out nesting species. A Big Day route is no more than a line drawn between feathered points.

"Go two-tenths of a mile. Stop at the pullout on the right. Listen for Canada and Magnolia warbler. Also Hooded."

Canada and Hooded. Check/Check.

"Do we have a backup for Maggie?"

"Next stop and one other location. Go three-tenths of a mile and pull off just in front of a large white pine. I had a creeper on Monday, also Maggie. This is where the Yellow-rumped nested three years ago."

"Three-tenths. Gotcha."

No serious Big Day effort in New Jersey builds its strategy around hitting migrant traps anymore. Why? Because they don't work—at least not often enough to make them worth the risk. They don't work, because the flood of migrants that used to sweep the state, that inspired Urner's Big Days, has been reduced to a sputtering trickle.

If Charles Urner and his cronies were to run their traditional Big Day route today, their total probably wouldn't crack 140. And the terrible silence that would greet them at their dawn site would shatter their immortal souls. Why, they might just wander home around midday, curl up into the fetal position, put their thumbs in their mouths, and rock back and forth.

Sometimes I want to do that myself.

There are birders who are disdainful of Big Days. They are frivolous and silly affairs, they say. They cheapen serious birding and reduce an aesthetic pursuit to a frenetic game. A Big Day, they lecture, doesn't have the utilitarian payoff of bird atlasing, or the potential conservation benefits of shorebird surveys or hawk counts.

And all these criticisms are valid. But it is wrong to say that Big Days are valueless. For one thing, they are fun, and in this age of this world, real fun is a very rare and very valuable thing. And for another, they offer historic perspective, a window to another age of birding, and a yardstick to measure change and loss.

There aren't twenty years of World Series of Birding team totals, but there are ten. And during the World Series there are multiple teams of skilled birders scouring the countryside with an intensity that makes Christmas Bird Counts look like a stroll through the park. In 1992 there were over fifty teams.

And if you look at all the team totals for the past ten years you find many of the birds that Urner took for granted just don't grow on trees any more.

For instance, Least Flycatcher, a bird never missed by Urner, has been recorded by only 50 percent of all World Series teams. Gray-cheeked Thrush, *never missed by Urner*, has been recorded by only 19 percent of all World Series teams.

Golden-winged Warbler, another bird with a 20/20 record, has been tallied by only 43 percent of all teams. And Worm-eating Warbler, missed by every third World Series team, was never missed by Urner.

And then there is Black-throated Blue . . . or, perhaps it is more accurate to say, then there *wasn't* Black-throated Blue.

We finished our 1990 Big Day with 210 species—a total beyond the reach of Urner's dreams. All it took was fifty-plus years of Big Day tradition, and the combined wisdom of seven previous World Series of Birding competitions. All it took was an interstate highway system to whisk us along and a Saab 9000 to whisk along in. All it took was five hundred person-hours of team scouting, one full-state dry run of our route, and 180 World Series of Birding participants all scouring the state and pooling their sightings prior to the May 19th Big Day.

Two hundred ten species. An auspicious total and an effortful one.

But the bird I remember most, the one that seems most enduring, is the bird that got away, the warbler that Urner never missed. Little Lost Blue. In the years to come, I will give much thought to that bird and what it suggests about birding's future.

Putting the "Good" in "Good Bird"

Of all the questions birders pose to birders, the one that stops me every time is also the one most commonly phrased: "Have you seen any 'good' birds?"

Now, I ask you, how do you go about fielding a loaded question like that? Just what puts the "good" in "good bird"?

Usually, I find myself not answering, not right away. I just stand there, impersonating a Yellow-crowned Night-Heron with tetanus. Part of me wants reach out to the errant soul, to offer an impromptu chickadee appreciation seminar. The other part wants to dislocate the kneecap on another snob birder trying to back me into a metaphysical corner.

"Just say no," my sainted wife Linda prompts. "Don't make a big deal out of it. Don't play Ghandi. Don't play Rambo. Just say . . ."

"No!" I scream (in my mind). "I haven't seen any *good* birds. Nothing but garbage. Nothing but trash birds. Chickadees and titmice and worthless, scruffy Song Sparrows." Brrrrrrr.

"How dare you impugn my appreciation of titmice with your fascist bird snobbery!" I dream of shouting. "Have I seen any *good* birds? Pah. I spit on your notion of good birds. I . . ."

But this is just a fantasy. "Why, yes," I hear myself saying, surrendering, quietly hating my ethical paralysis. "There's a Curlew Sandpiper feeding with Stilt Sandpipers over in the West Pool," I'll direct. Or "No, I haven't seen anything . . . 'good.'" Fact is, I occasionally catch myself asking this same stupid question when I meet other birders in the field, perpetuating this unjust system of avian segregation.

Why must good be synonymous with rare? Why does a bird have to be a thousand miles from where it belongs or heading for biological bankruptcy in order to be good?

Why can't the good in good bird relate to color and shape and design? That's what puts good in good art. Has anyone ever admired a Van Gogh because it was perched in a gallery four thousand miles from Arles? No. They admire it because it is great art.

Why can't the good in good bird relate to a bird's poise or performance? That's what puts the good in good acting. Nobody (except maybe Marlon Brando) has ever developed a reputation for good acting by turning up on a movie set about as often as Cox's Sandpipers turn up in Massachusetts.

Why can't the good in good bird relate to a bird's prowess or skill? That's what puts the good in a golfer's putt, a second baseman's play, a linebacker's charge.

I'm not the only one who has a problem meeting other people's expectations of a "good bird." I once saw Victor Emanuel, of Victor Emanuel Nature Tours, try to respond to the deadly demand in Cave Creek Canyon, Arizona.

Victor, a true Renaissance birder, responded by recounting encounters with Strickland's Woodpeckers, Elegant Trogons, Sulphur-bellied Flycatchers, and a "wonderful" Painted Redstart. Finding these species in southeastern Arizona is the birding equivalent of going to Mount Rushmore and finding the likenesses of Washington, Jefferson, Lincoln, and Roosevelt. But the woman who had posed the question regarded him as if he, Victor, were offering her the Brooklyn Bridge. These weren't "good birds" her expression said. These were everyday birds. She wanted to hear about *good* birds, like American Redstarts or Mountain Trogons, which *are* good birds. But no better than Painted Redstarts or Elegant Trogons.

What she wanted was to visit Mount Rushmore and see the Acropolis.

Listen, you want to see the Acropolis? Greece is your best

bet. I'll draw you a map. You want to see an American Redstart? What's wrong with Massachusetts? Mountain Trogon? Try Mexico.

I know I'm being overly simplistic about all this. I understand and appreciate the pleasure of watching birds that I rarely see—either because they are uncommon or because the species falls outside *my* normal range. But I'm also nervous about endorsing a system of values that puts an accent on avian paucity. If uncommon is good and rare is better, what does that make extinct?

And I'm not one to denigrate chickadees and titmice just because one of the charms accounted among their considerable attributes is consistency. A chickadee is just a good bird that I get to see all the time.

So, the next time someone poses the deadly demand and wants to know whether I've seen anything "good," I think I will reply, "Yes, all the usual good birds." And maybe hope that they don't press me for details.

The Talk of Sterile Flat

SCENE: *An observation tower overlooking a mud flat the size of Kansas. The tide is decidedly out. About three time zones away is a vibrating brown mass that might be shorebirds. The sun is . . . well, you guess.*

Three birders are standing on the tower. One is tall, spare, and tranquil as a rubber band held at full draw. His binoculars are German and new. His spotting scope with its three eyepieces costs 150,000 yen. The smudge on his polo shirt bespeaks his love of chocolate-filled croissants.

The second gentleman is older, tanned, and fit. He is mantling a telescope that resembles a locomotive boiler. His eye is fused to the stack.

The third is a kid. He could be a computer hacker or a mass murderer. It's difficult to say. The baseball cap labels him a Dodgers fan. The binoculars with the teeter-totter focus mechanism and the field guide poking from a hip pocket brand him a beginning birder.

RUBBERBAND (*pacing*): I think the tide's coming in now. What do you think? Do you think it's coming in? It's supposed to be.

BOILERMAN (*not looking up*): I guess so.

RUBBERBAND: Have you had anything good?

BOILERMAN: I got here just before you did.

TEETER-TOTTER (*butting in*): I been here since dawn. There was an Osprey carrying a fish. It was way close. It was awesome.

BOILERMAN: Oh, wait a minute, wait just a minute, I've got an interesting bird here. This one looks pretty good to me.

RUBBERBAND (*panning frantically*): What? Where?

BOILERMAN (*pensive, distracted*): On the right side of the back, middle group, feeding with Dun—

RUBBERBAND: I got it. I got it. Looks good to me. Good curve on the bill.

TEETER-TOTTER: Where is it again?

BOILERMAN (*hesitant*): Weeell, now I'm not so sure. It might look just like the bird next to it.

RUBBERBAND: Yeah. Yeah. I was just going to say that. The distance is terrible. It's the distance that makes it so tough.

TEETER-TOTTER: Where again?

RUBBERBAND: When was "the bird" last seen?

BOILERMAN: Yesterday.

TEETER-TOTTER: What bird?

RUBBERBAND: Here?

BOILERMAN: Right here . . . oh . . . oh . . . lookee here. Look at this little darlin' here. It's picture perfect. It's—

RUBBERBAND: I got it. Feeding. Facing left . . . now right . . . now left. Looks good. Good curve on that bill.

BOILERMAN: Weeell, I'm getting cold feet about it, now. It doesn't look as good as it did a minute ago.

RUBBERBAND (*sighs*): No. The bill is wrong. Should have more curve. It's looking into the sun that makes it so tough. (*He walks away from his scope. Walks back. Looks at his watch.*) The tide is getting better all the time, though. What do you think?

BOILERMAN (*not looking up*): I'm sure you're right.

TEETER-TOTTER: I dunno. I don't think that sandbar was visible before. Say, what are you guys looking for anyway? Somethin' radical?

RUBBERBAND (*tersely*): The tape bird. (*The kid's mouth draws a silent* O.)

RUBBERBAND (*addressing Boilerman*): Do you need it?

BOILERMAN: I need it here. But I got it in three other states.

RUBBERBAND (*chagrined*): Oh. Well . . . I need it.

TEETER-TOTTER (*casually scanning*): I guess I need it, too. Say, what's this bird over—

BOILERMAN: Sweet mercy! Bless me, but this one's snapshot perfe—

RUBBERBAND (*shouting*): I GOT IT. Saw it just before you called it out. That's it. Nice pick.

TEETER-TOTTER: No, I mean this bird over here by itself.

BOILERMAN: It does stand taller than the rest. Wish it would raise its head so we could see the bill.

TEETER-TOTTER: My bird's got its bill showing. It's bent way rad. The head's round like a marble.

RUBBERBAND: I think I can get some color on it. Yep! It *definitely* has color on the breast.

TEETER-TOTTER: This one's mostly white underneath . . . with a couple of red spots.

BOILERMAN: I got her at 140 × now. No, that's no good. That's awful. Just a brown blur.

TEETER-TOTTER: This one's brown on top, too. Except for where the tail attaches to the body.

RUBBERBAND: THERE! Its head's up! Great look! Perfect!

BOILERMAN: Hmmmmm. I don't know. I'm not so sure now.

RUBBERBAND (*disappointed*): I see what you mean. Damn! It's almost impossible with all these heat waves. It's the heat waves that make it so tough. Oh . . . It's up!

BOILERMAN: Damn. They're *all* up. (*turning*) Did you get a look at the rump?

RUBBERBAND (*hesitating*): Uh . . .ye—, well, no.

BOILERMAN: I didn't either. (*addressing the kid*) Did you?

TETTER-TOTTER (*apologetic, looking up from his field guide*): No. I was looking at another bird, but it flew.

BOILERMAN: Well, I don't think ours was the bird, now.

RUBBERBAND (*angry, pacing, glancing at his watch*): I guess I'm not sure either. I'll have to study some plates tonight. (*He walks away from his scope and looks at his watch again.*) Tide's looking better, though. What do you think?

BOILERMAN (*still scanning; not looking up*): Uh-huh.

RUBBERBAND: Better all the time. It's the waiting that's so bad. It's the waiting that makes it so tough.

[CURTAIN]

"Sterile Flat" is imaginary. The characters are fictions. The plot? Call it a worst-case scenario.

The Devil List

You can see them, sitting in the shadowed corners of the Anchorage Airport Hotel lounge, or hunched over tables at Al T's restaurant in High Island, Texas—North American bird listers.

Their days are long, their nights tortured by dreams of feathered waifs that touch and go. They thrive on rumor, live for whispers and a telephone ringing deep in the night.

" . . . Yes! The bird was there today. Seen on a rising tide. Absolutely no question about it. They're organizing a charter out of Kotzebue and there's a couple of seats left . . ."

But mostly they just nurse their warm beers and stir circles in pools of catsup with cold french fries. Waiting. Hoping.

Once they were vibrant and alive, just like you. They birded with enthusiasm and looked at cardinals. But that was before their lives were ruined by . . .

The Devil List!

How did this happen? How were these lives ruined and could it happen to you? The answer is yes. It can happen to anyone because it begins with innocence.

Think back! Remember how it was when *you* first started birding. How a window opened up to a world filled with color and song? How every day began with wonders and every evening was buoyed by the day's discoveries?

Do you remember how the little check marks began mounting in the margin of your field guide—tiny tokens of achievement, little building blocks of pride?

Do you recall how one day you counted them up and there

were fifty and this made you feel good? The next time you counted there were a hundred and this made you feel even better!

Beware! Before you know it, you too may be on the road to:

LISTING MADNESS!

Precisely what is "listing"? Well, it's nothing your parents would have told you about at the onset of puberty and nothing your grandmother even heard of. If you ask your closest birding friends about listing, they will assert—will *swear*—that *they* are not listers, *themselves.* (Nothing here but us aesthetically oriented chickadee mavens, right?) "But that guy over there . . ."

"What guy?"

"Shhhhh. *That* guy sitting over by the wall phone reading *British Birds.* I'm *sure* he's one. Now, you'll have to excuse me, I've got to go call the hotli—my hotel."

Listing, simply put, is the acquisition and enumeration of birds seen by an individual, a measure of achievement and skill.

American Robin . . . *tick!* Carolina Chickadee . . . *tick!* Eastern Phoebe . . . *tick*!

But what sometimes happens—not always, but sometimes—is that the distinction between skill (which is acquired) and the list (which is the measure of skill) becomes blurred. It *sometimes* happens that people lose their bearings and, instead of being a measure of birding skill, the list becomes birding's *objective.* Satisfaction no longer stems from discovering or identifying birds. It comes from adding more birds to the list. And more, and more, and more . . .

But like wealth, like power, more is not necessarily more satisfying. More is a cheat. More is an opiate. More only satisfies for a little while. It appeases, but it doesn't satiate. It only leaves you wanting . . .

More!

And more plays a little jest on birders, too. It poisons the process. Because the more birds a birder finds, why, the fewer there are *to* find and the harder it becomes to get the next one.

The *next* one. That is the important thing. Never mind all

the birds that came before. Never mind all the color and song. What is important is the next bird. The one that hasn't been seen, hasn't been run to ground.

The one that has eluded you. Cheated you. Mocks you every time you review your list and see the empty box next to the name.

The next one.

And when you find it, the thirst moves on . . . and on . . . and on, until the lure of the list not only controls your birding, it controls your life. Determines your vacations. Eats up your expendable income. Makes you miss family gatherings. Puts you on a first-name basis with car rental clerks in McAllen, Texas.

Until finally, one day—after your spouse has remarried, after your children have changed their names, after your unemployment insurance benefits have long since run out—you pick up your checklist and discover that all the little boxes are filled.

You stand at the far side of ambition and stare at a perfect list the way the pioneers might have stared at the Pacific Ocean—with a mixture of horror and frustration. And you look back across a continent stripped of discovery and wonder what it will be like to spend the rest of your days sitting in Al T's boring patrons with the story of your life Barnacle Goose.

And, now, you'll have to excuse me. I've got to go call a guy.

Keith Hansen 1993

Courting Disaster

He opened his eyes, shielded them with a raised hand and, squinting, studied the dial of his watch. It read a little after four. He'd slept for over an hour.

Not a good night to have to deal with a sunburn, a cautioning layer of consciousness counseled.

Better turn over, he thought.

He sat up, displaying the well-tempered body of a young man in his late twenties, pivoted lightly upon his beach towel and settled into prone recline. The bird was on him immediately.

"*Yrrrrrrch,*" the feathered missile screamed as it pulled up a feather's breadth from the man's head. "*Yrrrrrrch.*"

"Crazy bird!" he thought darkly, glancing over at the young woman lying beside him. Still asleep, he was pleased to see. The bird hadn't troubled her at all.

The man's glance assumed the properties of a gaze. Since the man was no longer moving, the bird broke off its attack and returned to its spot on the beach.

The problem with the bird, a tiny gray and white tern, had begun as soon as the couple had moved their towels higher up on the beach to avoid the incoming tide. All of a sudden, for no reason they could see, this bird had been all over them, screeching and dive-bombing.

At first they'd tried to drive it away with their beach towels. But the bird was too agile. It avoided the towels neatly. After a time, the couple realized that the bird was more annoyance than threat and decided to ignore it. Sure enough, in a few minutes, the bird settled onto the sand a few feet away and glowered at them with angry, black eyes. Only when one of the couple moved did the bird resume its attack.

The man's gaze broadened into a full-fledged stare. He studied the woman beside him and felt, once again, the constriction in his throat and tremor in his chest. They had met only a week ago—at the wedding of mutual friends—but the attraction had been instantaneous.

Just the way it happens in fairy tales, he thought. During the week, there had been telephone calls, flowers shipped to the office, and dinner—at a very exclusive restaurant uptown. It was during dessert, while the last of the wine was poured, that he had suggested a weekend at the shore, "at the parents' place."

"They aren't down for the season yet," he explained. "And there's lots of room," he added quickly.

She hadn't exactly hesitated. Hesitancy stems from uncertainty or lack of confidence and she was without these. It was more nearly a pause, like the calm that settles over the ocean as the tide changes.

"All right," she said, touching the wine glass to her lips, not looking away. This was the first time the tightness had gripped his chest.

Looking down at her now, he was certain that she was the smartest, most attractive, most desirable woman that he'd ever met. She was, in a word, wonderful.

He didn't want to let her see him staring and he didn't want to wake her yet. So he settled down onto the blanket and let his eyes play over the sky, the clouds, the waves, and the beach. They came to rest, finally, upon the kamikaze bird—not because he was particularly interested in birds, but because when something stares at you, it's hard not to stare back.

The feathered dart fidgeted. Sometimes it would approach on its comically short legs, then nervously edge away again. Ever so often, the bird would vocalize—a single muttered call of anger or frustration.

What was this thing's problem? the man pondered.

Overhead and a little farther up the beach there were other

terns, a colony. Some were sitting in the sand, their bodies half hidden in shallow depressions. Only the pale gray backs, night-black caps, and bright yellow bills were visible. These were adult birds.

Other terns were standing by the water's edge. Most were not as handsome as the ones reclining on the beach. Their caps were not as sharp or full; their plumage, mottled, natty. These were subadults—nonbreeding birds.

But many terns, perhaps half of the colony, were aloft, and if birds can dance, then these danced, filling the air with the excited chatter of terns locked in the great ritual of courtship. Two birds, larger but otherwise very similar to the rest, flew by on scimitar wings. With the practiced precision of paired figure skaters, they set their wings, arched their backs, lowered their heads, and parachuted in tandem, chattering excitedly. The movement was exquisite. Their timing perfect.

It was spring. The season of procreation. But before procreation comes courtship—that delicate, but universal, ritual of breaking barriers and forming bonds.

"What time is it?" the woman asked suddenly.

"Four-thirty," the man replied, raising his hand, glancing at his watch. The bird was on him immediately.

"*Yrrrrch,*" it screamed, passing close enough to the man to make him duck his head. "*Yeeeerch.*"

"So our friend is still here," the woman said, opening her eyes, turning over on her stomach.

"Yep," the man replied (hoping that the woman hadn't seen him duck). "He really seems to have it in for us," he added as the bird returned to the beach. "It's like something out of a Hitchcock movie."

"Do you like movies?" she asked.

"I *love* movies," he assured her.

"Fellini? Bergman?"

"Absolutely," he affirmed (wondering who the hell Fellini was).

There was silence for a time as they both studied the bird who was studying them. It was the first silence that had fallen between them.

"You don't suppose the bird has a nest around here do you?" she asked suddenly.

"There isn't a tree in sight," her companion asserted.

"Don't some types of birds nest on beaches?" she asked.

"Yeah. Real dumb ones," he replied, trying to sound clever (and failing badly).

As they watched, a second tern flew in and lit near the first. In its beak was a small silver-sided fish. It approached the first bird on mincing feet, offering the fish. The first bird, the female, refused.

Only at this point did the bird bearing the fish seem to notice the two human intruders. It flew toward them, hovering a few feet over their heads.

"*Yuuuurch,*" it scolded. "*Yuuuuurch*" (which is "*yeeeerch*" when it is filtered through a fish). Its eviction efforts a failure, the bird returned to the female, who after several moments of coaxing finally accepted the fish. Moments later, the birds flew off, together. She led; he followed.

"What do you think about dinner?" the man offered.

"I think it sounds wonderful," the woman replied (accentuating the "wonder" in wonderful).

"I know a terrific seafood restaurant here in town. Do you like seafood?"

"I *love* seafood," she affirmed, hiding her disappointment well. She had hoped he'd suggest one of the small, chic cafes.

"What do you say we pack up?" he said, rising, offering her a hand.

"Fine," she said, taking it.

Together they collected their belongings, grabbed the cooler, shook the sand out of their towels, and left with their hands joined and the surf clutching at their ankles.

Left without ever seeing the sand-colored egg nestled in the shallow depression that had miraculously escaped their paraphernalia and their feet. Not that it mattered. The tiny Least Tern egg was beyond salvage, even by miracles, now. Four hours' exposure to the hot spring sun had seen to that.

The Wisdom of the Worthies

I finished reading the March 1992 copy of *Feathering It,* newsletter of the Arithmetickers Birding Alliance—in which members debated the avisophical question "Do heard-only birds count?"—and sighed. Respondents were hopelessly divided on the issue, leaving me troubled and no closer to a resolution of *my* problem.

Reverently, I reached for my life list, running a finger down the ranks of sight-sanctified entries. Feeling good, feeling proud, feeling pure-at-heart—until my finger came to rest upon the cold, dark blemish in my list, my character, and my soul.

The Black Rail! Accounted right there among the other entries even though it was no more than a "kick-ee-doo" in the night.

Propelled by anxiety, driven by guilt, I decided to take my moral dilemma down to the Cedarville diner to invoke the wisdom of the town worthies. Here, every morning at seven, the world's problems are laid out beside eggs over easy and hash browns. Here they are thoughtfully chewed, digested, and [judgment] passed.

Certainly, I reasoned, people who can tell the president how to fix the economy and Lee Iaccoca how to build his pickup trucks to run like a Ford should be able to tell me something as simple as whether birds that are identified by their calls but not seen should count on my life list.

"Count fer what?" Bob Henschel, a local dairyman, demanded.

"You know," I said, "count."

"They can count on me to dust their grubby little asses with shot if they don't stay out of my grapes," observed Phil Sayre, one of the county's most respected farmers.

"Look at the lilies of the field and the birds of the air," the Reverend John C. Johns intoned, forking a chunk of hash browns into his mouth, using the silence to dramatize his somewhat oblique point. "They do no work, yet the good lord provides for them."

"That's a fact," Phil said. "Near as I can tell they don't work a lick—just sit in my fields and steal my crops."

"Excuse me, fellahs," I interrupted, "but you don't understand. What I mean is, do heard birds count?"

"Nope," Bob Henschel said flatly. "Been raising cows all my life and never known them black- and brown-headed herd birds to account fer nothing."

I took a deep breath but it was Alan Corson, bayman and four-term mayor, who spoke up first.

"Henschel," he said, "you're gettin' dumber than them cows you tend. He don't want to know whether birds count fer something, he wants to know whether birds can count, like ciphering figures. An' I don't know 'bout other birds, but I can tell you fer a fact that ducks can count, 'cause as soon as I shoot my limit, the rest of 'em just swarm all over my decoys."

"'Course they can count," Phil added in agreement. "If birds couldn't count, what'd be the sense in getting in a group. Might as well stay by yourself—and listen, Mister, how come you keep sayin' 'herd'? I thought a mess o' birds all standin' around together was called a flock."

"You're right," I affirmed, thinking that maybe we were making progress now, "flock. But I'm not interested in birds counting; I'm interested in counting birds—like in a list. What I want to know is, can you count a bird on a list if you just hear it or do you have to see it, too?"

"Oh," four voices intoned, as four sets of eyes went flat and unfocused—and it is a credit to how seriously this august assembly takes the problems of the world that not one of the gentlemen present asked "What for?" (although it certainly must have occurred to them).

"But of course they count," Rev. John said, recovering first. Metaphysical matters were his specialty, and besides, if people stopped putting credence in what they heard, he'd be out of a job.

"Remember that God spoke to Moses, who listened and took his people out of Egypt."

Bob and Alan nodded but Phil didn't buy it.

"Now hold on there, Reverend. God used to back up his audio with some pretty nifty special effects—burning bushes and believable stuff like that. I say a man just can't go along believin' everything he hears. He does that, why, he'll end up buyin' newspapers over the phone or votin' Democratic or sumthin'. I say a man can't never count on sumthin' he don't see with his own two eyes, includin' birds."

The minister leaped to a rebuttal, but his argument was cut short by a snarl from waitress Shirley Dockerty, who let it be known that she'd been handing the lot of them very legible bills for fifteen years and not one of them had managed to count out the right amount of change yet.

Then another patron wanted to know whether "bills" were the same as "beaks." Then some guy named Arty started to describe this bird "with a real long neck . . ."

I stuck around until John and Phil started arguing about the tree that falls in the forest—and whether you have to see the tree that falls (even though you aren't there to hear it) in order to prove that it was a tree that did (or did not) make any sound. Then, with no one taking any particular notice, I said thank you and goodby and went home to shred my life list.

Keith Hansen 1993

Hide and Seek

It would take something keener than the human eye to detect anything but leaves and shadows. It would take even more than the eye of a hunting hawk to pick out the small, olive-colored bird perched within the canopy—unless the bird moved. Movement catches a hunting eye like a flare on a moonless night.

There was no shortage of hunting eyes, either. Overhead, a river of Sharp-shinned Hawks was flowing south—hundreds, thousands. Weaving a course through the maze of branches were other Sharp-shinneds whose focus had shifted from migration to active hunting.

Hide and seek is an old game with Sharp-shinneds. As the astonishing number of raptors overhead attests, they are pretty accomplished gamesters.

In an adjacent field, several Northern Harriers were patrolling for incautious meadow voles or songbirds. Harriers tend to be pretty eclectic about these things. On scattered perches, half a dozen Merlins and one very hungry male Peregrine surveyed the landscape and over every likely looking patch of vegetation an American Kestrel hovered.

Instruments of vireo demise seemed everywhere. About the only thing that the vireo didn't have to worry about was the immature Bald Eagle perched on a nearby snag. Eagles are not very adept at catching birds whose weight is measured in grams.

The hard truth was that the woodlands north of Cape May

Point, New Jersey, are a very rough neighborhood for songbirds who seek to maintain their membership among the ranks of living things. Short of digging a burrow or slipping into a flak jacket (both of which vireos are ill equipped to do) staying hidden and immobile was not a bad strategy for survival. In fact, as strategies go, it had only one major failing. It didn't address the vireo's food needs—which were severe.

Migration is energy taxing. Feeding is a simple way of dealing with this problem, but feeding means having to move—which given the circumstances was not an attractive prospect. It was certainly a dilemma, a paradox.

The bird, the immature Red-eyed Vireo, didn't have to analyze the problems she faced or devise a solution. The bird already *knew* everything she needed to know about the problem, including how to deal with it. She knew because she was the product of a long line of survivors who had dealt with this problem and succeeded. The prize for winning the game is the right to pass on the secret of your success to the next generation.

Part of the bird's success was tied to plumage. The vireo's wings and back were olive green, the color of leaves in shade. Immobile, the bird was just another dark patch in a collage whose medium was leaf and shadow.

The bird's underparts were pale yellow-white, but with the bird hunkered down on a limb, out of direct sunlight, there was nothing to distinguish her from the many splashes of sunlight among the leaves, nothing to catch and hold a hunting eye.

The effectiveness of the bird's disguise had been put to the test several times already since she had dropped into the willow-oak shortly after dawn. Nearly a dozen Sharp-shinneds had passed within ten feet. Two had momentarily perched in the same tree. One hunting Sharp-shinned had surprised and captured an immature Blackpoll Warbler that was foraging on the branch the vireo rested upon.

As the vireo contemplated her options (if "contemplated" is the right word) another Sharp-shinned Hawk approached. The vireo watched the agile predator weave a path through the branches, its long tail maneuvering the bird through air the way a rudder moves a boat in the water. Barely a leaf was troubled as the bird slipped through the leafy maze.

If the vireo was immobile before, she was paralyzed now. The Sharp-shinned passed within four feet, and for one terrible moment, the vireo could see her reflection in the yellow gaze of the hawk. But the vireo went unrecognized. The disguise had passed another test and another round in the game of hide and seek went to the vireo.

The Sharp-shinned Hawk moved on in search of birds less adept (or less fortunate).

The end of immediate danger seemed to galvanize the vireo to action. Her food needs had finally gotten the upper hand, and although movement was risky, failing to refuel was suicide. Any vireo that didn't reach the tropics before cold weather was a failure and the penalty for failure is simple. Failures don't get to breed in the spring.

The bird made a single, short hop to a lower limb. She didn't flutter. She didn't even open her wings. She simply dropped, the way a leaf might—dropping and catching up on a lower branch. Very simple. Very natural. There, she waited.

Nothing. No blur of wings. No yellow eyes. No clutching talons. Another success story.

The bird moved again. A lateral hop to an adjacent limb. Nothing again.

The bird's slow, stop-and-go movements reveal another secret to vireo success. When movement is unavoidable, don't make any sudden moves. Above all, avoid any movement that does not appear *natural.*

Here's another little tip, a fine point of survival: Pick your perches with care. A little shadow never hurts.

Vireos are careful, methodical feeders, using stealth to buffer risk. Other birds employ other strategies. Some flock to lose themselves in the anonymity of the pack. Some rely on superior reflexes or speed. There are many strategies, but they all have at least one thing in common—they all work well enough to maintain the species.

Does this mean that the vireo had nothing to worry about? No. You see, Sharp-shinned Hawks are a successful species, too.

The young vireo saw a fat green caterpillar hidden under a leaf. Its green color was almost a perfect replication of the top side of the leaf—but unfortunately for the caterpillar, not the paler underside of the leaf. Vireos love caterpillars.

The vireo foraged outward toward the edge of the tree, toward the sunlight. It was a cool morning. Insects, as cold-blooded creatures, were more common and more active where the temperatures were higher.

The vireo found another caterpillar and ate it. She missed two more whose camouflage defeated her eyes, then located a third. Pickings were pretty slim.

The feeding activity of a dozen other birds (including several vireos) attracted our bird. Several species of migrating songbirds were gorging themselves on a multicolored stand of porcelain berries not far away.

Vireos love porcelain berries, too.

In one sense, the risk was greater since the berries were in plain view, exposed to sunlight and hunting eyes. But the returns were greater, too. The bird would be able to feed quickly (reducing risk) and since food was plentiful, she wouldn't have to move about much (also reducing risk). It seemed like a fair trade-off, and besides, the hawks appeared to be flying much higher than they had earlier. Most were migrating; few seemed intent on hunting now.

The vireo flew across the clearing, landed amid the berries, and began to feed. More birds, noting the activity, joined the feeding flock. It was too much to hope that this kind of activity would go unnoticed forever.

The Cooper's Hawk, another bushwacker and one that might be likened to the big brother of a Sharp-shinned, ducked into the canopy to come at the birds from behind. A Blue Jay screamed a warning. Vireos and warblers scattered.

The vireo, intent on evading the Cooper's Hawk, didn't see the diving Sharp-shinned until it was too late. The vireo managed one desperate barrel roll which the Sharpy followed easily. Then, with reflexes too fast to contemplate, the Sharp-shinned reached out and closed the vireo in a net of talons.

The Cooper's Hawk hit the Sharp-shinned with enough force

to break the raptor's grasp, and send the vireo spiraling upward. She righted herself and fled for the protecting veil of leaves, narrowly evading another Sharp-shinned en route. The Cooper's Hawk, flying heavily, carried the hapless Sharp-shinned Hawk into the trees.

Luck plays a crucial role in success, too—both good luck and bad.

Five minutes later, her panic over, the vireo was once again feeding on the porcelain berries. Life must go on.

On the tip of a branch, just over her head, she spied another caterpillar. She stretched to reach it but came up short. She tried again and failed again. She tried once more, fluttering her wings to give herself the extra boost she needed.

The wings caught the sunlight and, against the dark backdrop of the leaves, they flickered like a flare on a moonless night. The bird opened her bill. Success was almost hers.

Vireos love caterpillars. As much as Sharp-shinneds love vireos.

Keith Hansen
1993

Snowy Reprieve

By noon the crowd in front of Bob Ellis' yard had turned the snow to slush and threatened the integrity of Agatha Cromley's flower garden. They even had to send a patrolman down to keep traffic moving along the usually quiet street. Seeing the crowd, and assuming the worst, several volunteer firemen had stopped to lend assistance. Even after learning their mistake, they stayed to share the excitement and holiday atmosphere.

Bob Ellis, Jr., bemoaned the loss of snow but found the notoriety just compensation. Yes, it was he, he admitted to the reporter, who had discovered the bird. "Right there," he said, pointing to the gabled roof over his bedroom. There was no denying the accuracy of his assertion. The large white owl with the catlike gaze was plain to see. The owl, its yellow eyes drawn to narrow slits, regarded the crowd with detachment. The bird had long ago concluded that the noisy assemblage posed no threat. Even the several snowballs thrown by future neighborhood all-stars had earned no more than its passing notice.

Of far greater interest to the owl were Agatha Cromley's orange tabby, who was busy stalking sparrows at the bird feeder, and the flock of heckling crows that had temporarily withdrawn to the nearby steeple of St. Paul's church. Though the crows and cat lay in opposite directions, the bird could monitor both by simply rotating its head—a feat that brought repeated gasps from spectators and futile attempts at mimicry by assorted preschoolers.

The day had begun magically enough for Bob, Jr., though the evening before had been pure hell. He had gone to bed nearly sick with anxiety. Over and over again he'd promised his soul to servile bondage to any god that might be monitoring the heaven-sent aspirations of fourth-graders—and who could pile up enough snow to make them close down school for the day.

The impending storm was going to be a cliff-hanger, a real squeaker. The weatherman was only calling for an accumulation on the order of four to eight inches. Four inches, Bob knew from sad experience, wouldn't be enough. His school system was the stingiest and most mean-spirited in the whole district. His school system was *always* the last to cancel classes on account of snow. Always. It was going to take *at least* eight inches of the white stuff.

"I mean, it's just not fair," he had argued at the dinner table the night before, trying to make his parents see the monstrous injustice of it all. "All the private school kids get off every time there's a heavy frost, for Cripes' sake. *We* have to go to school even when it's snowin' a blizzard. *We'd* have to go to school even if there was another ice age. Do you call that fair?"

It certainly wasn't fair, but as injustices go, it didn't differ much from a billion other injustices Bob would confront in the course of his life. Knowing this, and knowing that only time can communicate this sort of understanding, Bob's parents had listened patiently, advised him to hope for the best but prepare for the worst—then turned their thought to the injustices that besieged their own lives: bills and taxes and clothes that fit too snugly (things that even the magic inherent in snow cannot change).

By bedtime, the snow had still not started and Bob's anxiety levels had reached life-threatening proportions. "I guess I'll just get up early and do that stupid report—if I have to," he lied. He went to sleep wondering how to get even with gods so stingy that they won't even send a kid a little well-deserved snow now and again.

During the night he awakened to the sound of wind in the branches and the sound of feathery flakes beating against the windows like soft, white wings. In the morning, the first thing he heard was the blessed sound of the siren on the town hall sounding reprieve. The first thing he saw when he leaped to the window was ten inches of fulfilled promise, gleaming white and untouched by the hand of man or snowplow.

Quite predictably and understandably, all promises of servitude were forgotten. But it would have been an extremely naive god to have expected more.

It was the crows that tipped Bob off, betraying the Arctic visitor. The neighborhood boasted a small, suburbanized troop of American Crows who made a good living retrieving half-eaten doughnuts and punishing residents who failed to put the lids on their garbage cans. They also had it in for Agatha Cromley's cat, but this was just a hobby. All through breakfast the troop had maintained one hell of a racket, and by the sound of it, they had been reinforced by at least a division.

A "murder" had been the word his grandfather was fond of using. "A murder of crows."

Bundled for adventure, drawn by curiosity, Bob had minced his way into the yard, hating to be the one to mar the pristine whiteness. Turning and looking toward the roof, he discovered half a dozen crows screaming crazed insults at what appeared to be a small, soot-flecked snowman balanced on the roof. Without warning, the top of the lump swiveled and two piercing, yellow eyes pinned Bob to the snow.

Bob, Jr., hesitated barely a moment. Years of training had taught him precisely how to handle situations like this.

"Mom!" he shouted as he sprinted for the door.

"It's a Snowy Owl. The biggest owl in North America," he explained first to the neighbors, then to their friends, and as the morning progressed to more and more people who heard the news and came to see the rare Arctic visitor that had come with the snow. "Scientists call it *Nicotine sciatica,*" Bob continued, which was a pretty fair stab at the unfamiliar Latin name (considering that until just that morning this obscure bit of lore had lain dormant in the encyclopedia). "It eats lemmings mostly, and only leaves the Arctic when the lemmings disappear and it gets real hungry," he said, summarizing the rest of his newly acquired knowledge concerning Snowy Owls (*Nyctea scandiaca*). This was greeted with considerable relief by several young mothers . . . but Agatha Cromley, whose defense of her begonia patch was heroic, wasn't entirely won over by the arguments put forth by science.

Bob's recounting of the Snowy Owl's feeding and dispersal habits was only moderately flawed. The Arctic owls do indeed eat lemmings—and a good many other birds and mammals, too. And Snowy Owls do vacate the Arctic in numbers when lemming populations fall to the low point in their cycle. But a few birds, mostly immature, wander south every winter. The bird atop Bob Ellis' house was one of these. After the unwarranted concern for the safety of children was assuaged, it turned to the welfare of the bird. No, everyone agreed, the bird hadn't moved all day. Maybe it was sick or injured? Maybe it was hungry? Somebody suggested buying it some ground beef; someone else suggested calling the fire department, another the zoo . . . the S.P.C.A. . . . the Aw-doo-bon Society. Debate was furious.

But among the many experts present, it was the one not consulted, the one whose authority in these matters was absolute, whose decision held sway. "Look," Bob, Jr., shouted above the din, "It's gone." And so it was, except that the owl with the catlike gaze lived very much in his dreams for many nights thereafter.

As, in fact, it did in the simple mind of Agatha Cromley's tabby, who for the rest of his long and fortunate life never did willingly set foot in the snow or so much as look sideways at a bird feeder again.

On Thursday, the local weekly paper gave a full-page account of the rare visitor from the Arctic who had touched the lives of many in the town but whose errant passage was beyond both their grasp and their best misguided intention.

Spanning the Gulf with a Wing

The Higbee Beach parking area was stripped of vehicles—a bad sign. On the second week in October, even at midweek, the place should have been packed . . . *unless,* of course, there were no birds.

Like I said, bad sign.

In fact, there was only one other vehicle in the lot, a station wagon that was foreign to me. After ten years in Cape May, I had gotten to know just about everybody's car. This one, and its occupant(s), were beyond my ken.

But the six-car caravan strung out in the rearview mirror was very familiar, members of my birding workshop group. Some were New Jersey residents, some kindred souls from distant parts. *All* were avid birders lured to Cape May for a week of birding at the linchpin of autumn migration. I was their leader.

Judging by the signs, though, they'd be better off with a magician. Higbee Beach looked pretty quiet this morning—a regular avian desert. It was going to take a Houdini-class act to pull an interesting morning's birding out of this hat.

"OK," I pronounced, kicking into leader mode. "Here's how we're going to bird this course. Leave your scopes in the car. Don't forget your water bottles . . ."

As I laid down the ground rules, two figures cloaked in camouflaged coveralls cleared the trailhead, heading for the parked station wagon. In their right hands were equally well camouflaged shotguns. In the left, each brandished a very dead goose—a Canada and a Snow.

Deep inside, a stifled sigh sought an escape route. *Why a Snow Goose?* I thought quietly. *The situation is going to be touchy enough without having to fight a rearguard action with Paul Gallico. Why did they have to nail a Snow Goose?*

Birders and hunters are estranged groups. Though they have much in common, on many different levels, they are estranged. Life and death stands between them and very few bridges can span such a gulf.

Birders are hard-pressed to understand what it is that attracts hunters to their sport. "What possible attraction," they want to know, "can a dead bird have over a live one?"

Hunters, for their part, are suspicious of birders and some are downright derisive, regarding bird watching as a childish imitation of their sport—hunting with all the guts cut out of it.

Neither camp is particularly comfortable in the company of the other. If by chance a hunter and birder meet in the field, there may be a mumbled greeting or a perfunctory nod. More often, there is cold silence, averted eyes, awkwardness, even belligerence.

I think of two male dogs meeting on a common street, stiff-legged and bristling. I think of John James Audubon, who birded over the barrels of his fowling piece. I think of Aldo Leopold, who may have been the last great naturalist with the wisdom and the understanding to bridge the gap.

The hunters observed our group from the far side of the parking area, sizing us up. I can't say with certainty what went through their minds. But if their expressions were a window to their thoughts, the two seemed somewhat sheepish. Their uneasiness manifested itself in the speed with which they began loading their car. They did not look at us and spoke to each other in hushed tones. One said something inaudible, making an almost imperceptible nod in our direction with his head. The other laughed—a short, loud laugh. A nervous laugh.

There was no avoiding the pair. They had parked right next to the entrance gate. As my workshop group turned, I watched the faces of my students, noting how each assessed the situation and the scene.

One looked puzzled, wondering perhaps what hunters were

doing in a prime birding area. On several faces jaw muscles tightened, eyes darted quickly from the birds to the men and back to the birds again. Someone behind me uttered the predictable pronouncement: "Oh, the poor things." The words seemed to act as a chilling catalyst. Suddenly everyone had a pronouncement to make, some softly, some loudly, none of them complimentary. Had the hunters heard?

The tightened jaws, the narrowed eyes, and the long, studied look that passed between them was evidence enough. It was certain that all the pieces on the board were quickly moving toward an ugly exchange.

I acted without any plan or much thought. Bridges could wait. But it was clear that if a confrontation was to be avoided, what was needed was a buffer or a mediator, and the task seemed to fall to . . .

"Hi," I said, raising my right hand—an ancient gesture of friendship and appeasement. See. I hold no weapon.

"Hello," one said, gruffly. The other merely nodded. I concentrated on the verbal one.

"Nice birds," I observed, indicating the geese. Is that what waterfowlers say to each other? I wondered. It's what birders say. Maybe "Congratulations" is more in keeping with the proper vernacular.

"Thanks," the verbal one acknowledged.

The group had come to a halt behind me. The hunters stood waiting. Now what? I had to say something, even if just to hold the podium, to keep someone else from saying something that might touch off an explosion.

"Would you mind if I showed my group one of your birds?" I blurted. Don't ask me why.

Maybe the question was motivated by some logic more basic than thought. The birds, after all, were the objects that both camps had in common. In any negotiations step number one is: Seek common ground. At the same time, the birds were also the point of contention, the thing that had to be dealt with.

But in reflection, I am inclined to think that the question was motivated by *interest,* not instinct. I knew that *I* was drawn to the birds, fascinated by their uncommon proximity. I knew that *I* would appreciate the opportunity to study them closely and at leisure—the way Audubon and Wilson once did. The way all bird enthusiasts did before optics supplanted the fowling pieces in the hands of ornithologists.

But motive made little difference now. The offer was on the table; the fat was in the fire, for sure. How would the hunters react to such a bizarre request? How would my group react? What would the outcome be? It was too close to call.

The hunter hesitated, clearly taken aback. "Sure," he said, finally, tentatively, not at all sure what this was committing him to. Then he gestured toward the birds, inviting my choice.

I picked up the Canada (no sense pushing my luck). It was much lighter than I expected, somehow; still warm, still retaining the fabric, if not the form, of a living bird, it wasn't shot up badly. For this small gift, I allowed a sigh to escape.

"All right," I shouted in a general call to muster. "Everybody gather around. Introduction to Bird Topography 101. You don't get many opportunities like this one."

With more eagerness than I expected, the group closed around. Like a draftsman displaying a blueprint or Hippocrates addressing his students, I spread a wing on the backdrop of the hood and started lecturing.

"These long outer feathers are primaries, the inner ones are the secondaries. Do you see how the tips actually turn in different directions: primaries out, secondaries in?"

There were nods all around. This was better than any two-dimensional diagram. This was real.

"These long, pointed feathers closest to the body are the tercials. And if you look on the upper surface you see the wing coverts. Greater, median, lesser . . ."

More nods, accompanied by noises of interest and understanding. A hand reached out. Someone touched a wing tip. Someone else explored the coverts. Suddenly I realized that the hunters, too, had drawn close and were sitting in on the lecture. Their interest had been captured, too.

Synchronous molt, feather wear, stress lines—topics difficult to grasp through erudition and difficult to see through optics were made simple with the bird in hand.

The bridge formed by a bird's wing lasted less than five minutes. Lecture completed, questions answered, I put the bird back next to its companion as the group started down the trail.

"Thanks," I said, to the hunters.

"Don't mention it," the talkative one intoned.

"Good luck," the other hunter offered.

"Thanks," I said again. "We say: 'Good birding.' "

"Oh," he said, a little sheepishly. "Well, good birding then."

I walked quickly to catch up to my group thinking many things. The bridge formed by a bird's wing was gone now, it was true. But somehow the gulf didn't seem as wide as it had before.

Dialogue with the Godfather

It seemed that the parking lot was crowded, but my eyes wouldn't leave the lone figure standing on the hawk-watch platform. There was something about the posture, something in the way the figure brought his binoculars to bear, something about the chiseled silhouette of the man that made me lean forward . . . and hold my shock in check.

"No," the detached and rational part of my mind counseled, *"that is impossible."*

"But I know this man," I insisted. "It is he."

"Uh-uh," the oracle of my logic asserted. *"The man is dead. It is quite impossible.*

"A look-alike," the voice suggested. *"A simple matter of shared traits,"* it hypothesized. *"A prime example of subconscious association,"* it concluded. *"Recent studies have shown that the incidence of two individuals sharing similar or identical . . ."*

The figure on the platform turned then, and from across the parking lot I could see the unmistakable, patrician face; the pale gray eyes; the ridge-sharpened features creased by countless morning suns. With a smile, he brought his hand up in greeting.

" . . . So you see," the fact-crippled, reality-clouded portion of my brain summarized, *"it is quite impossible for this man to be Maurice Broun, Hawk Mountain's first curator."*

"Fine," I said. "You win. Now why don't you go balance a checkbook or remember a phone number while I go up and say hello to an old friend? I haven't seen him since he died." I started across the parking lot, understandably grateful for the sound of gravel underfoot.

"Hello," the figure called, in tones to match the warmth of his handshake. "What do you think prospects are for a good hawk flight today?"

"Hello, Maurice," I said, wholeheartedly but cautiously. Caution dictated that I ignore the invitation to talk shop until a few things got sorted out. "It's been a long time," I invited.

"Has it?" he said, and his eyes crinkled with mischief. "I'm not in a position to judge," he observed.

"I guess not," I agreed. "You haven't aged a bit, either," I added, building my acceptance of this unlikely scenario one step at a time.

"No," he said, "I haven't. It's one of the advantages," he added, declining to bring the subject of time to bear on me. A diplomatic kindness.

In his unaged face I saw the image of the twenty-five-year-old boy I was when we first met, right here at Cape May Point. But where time runs rivulets off of memories and those whose lives have run their course, it is corrosive to living flesh. Spirit or no, it was Maurice, and not I, who could see the changes the years had worked—unless, of course, I was bold enough to seek the truth reflected in his eyes.

"Maurice," I said, "you don't mind if I maintain a little skepticism about this meeting, do you?"

"No," he assured, "perfectly understandable. In fact, I'd be disappointed if you didn't."

"You know," I continued, "this whole scenario is pretty improbable. Why shouldn't I just write it off as a hoax or a dream?"

"Being skeptical is one thing," the old master admonished, "being pigheaded is another. Preconceptions cloud observations. Why don't you just take it all in and sort things out later?"

"All right," I agreed. "That seems reasonable enough."

"Speaking of improbability," Maurice observed wryly, "it's pretty improbable that you and I are the only people standing up here on this platform at the peak of the hawk migration. But here we are and here they aren't," he said, indicating the vacant platform with his hand.

There was no denying the accuracy of *this* observation, but, as evidence, it hardly built a case in support of having a conversation with a man who had died in 1978. Still, Maurice's advice seemed sound. There didn't seem any harm in just riding this dream or hallucination or spiritual encounter to a conclusion and panning it for substance later. Besides, it had been a long time since we'd talked (and who knows when I'd get another chance to converse with the man who invented hawk watching).

Suddenly, Maurice brought his old pair of Leitz binoculars up, focused, and shouted: "Merlin!" I turned, finding the stubby falcon as it crested a dune; the surreal blue upperparts sprayed sunlight in its wake.

"Beautiful," the Godfather pronounced. "Simply beautiful. We don't get many Merlins where I watch from. They stick closer to the coast like they do down here. The ones we *do* get tend to fly low. It's tough picking them up against the backdrop."

"Do you get much of a flight?" I asked, surprised.

"Yes indeed," he confided, "a terrific flight. All the birds that ever were," he added softly.

"Passenger Pigeons?" I asked hopefully.

"They darken the heavens," he noted, somberly.

"Eastern Anatum Peregrines?" I added, my enthusiasm rising.

"All that ever were," he repeated, grimly. The words disappeared in the chill air, leaving a hollow place where they had been.

I shuddered, trying to shake off the cold image painted by a dead man.

"Well, raptor populations have recovered, now," I said to change the subject, to put some warmth back in the conversation.

"Except for the Eastern Anatum," I added in response to the eyebrow that cocked like the hammer of a hawk gunner's scatter gun. "I don't suppose you got the latest Hawk Migration Association newsletter?" I inquired.

"No," Maurice confirmed. "I'm afraid my life membership has lapsed."

"Well," I continued enthusiastically, enjoying the role of tutor to the master, "just about everyone has been setting records in hawk counts recently. Broad-winged Hawk totals almost went off the board last year. Peregrines set records all up and down the East Coast. Cooper's Hawks did well. Merlins were stacked up like casino chips on Saturday night."

Maurice was silent, his eyes the color of February rains. Instead of being affected by my enthusiasm, he seemed saddened by the spilling of current events.

"Hawk Mountain had a banner year, too," I confirmed, thinking that perhaps his silence was rooted in my failure to give an accounting of his mountain.

But Maurice remained silent. The rain in his eyes turned slowly to ice and behind them a cold emptiness was growing—an emptiness that lies beyond rumor, beyond sane contemplation.

"So," he said, breaking into my monologue, "they still stand on their ridges and rooftops and count off passing hawks like they were soup cans rolling down a chute."

A protest rose in my throat, but it foundered in confusion and was cut off as Maurice continued.

"I wouldn't doubt that people have reached the point that they believe raptor populations wouldn't have recovered unless there was somebody standing out there to count them. Good heavens," he said, shaking his head.

I was stunned. This was the man who had clambered up onto a shotgun-shattered ridge top in Pennsylvania in 1934 and pioneered hawk watching. It was he, *he,* who had initiated the longest-running hawk count on record, the count he had personally conducted for thirty-two years. The record has never been equaled.

"But . . . Maurice," I stammered, "I thought you were the greatest hawk counter that ever lived."

The ice behind his eyes became a glacier. The dark loneliness expanded until its icy fingers found the hollow place in my ribs and squeezed until the ache went clear to my throat.

"Is that how people remember me?" he asked slowly, thoughtfully. "How very sad. How very much like the living. You know," he observed thoughtfully, "accuracy would be better served if history were written by the dead. All we have, after all, is our memories. We shepherd them against inaccuracy because they *are* all we have.

"The greatest hawk counter that ever lived," he repeated. "Well, I decline the honor and the title. What I *was,*" he asserted, "was a conservationist, a raptor protectionist. My life was used up in the protection and preservation of birds of prey.

"If I counted hawks," he continued, "it was as a tool to serve my ends and as a *means* of bringing people to a higher environmental awareness. How sad," he observed, "that people should have made a religion of the means and forgotten the ends."

"Are you saying, Maurice, that people shouldn't monitor the hawk migration? That it's all just a waste of time?"

He smiled again, the pale ghost of a smile. "Heavens no," he said almost lightly, "of course you should go on counting hawks. How else are succeeding generations going to trace the decline? How else will people in the next century be able to review the route humanity followed into a sterile, lifeless world?

"As for whether that is a waste of time or not," he added, suddenly grim, "that depends on your motives. If you are counting hawks merely to monitor their decline, keep it up. If you're doing it under the incredible misapprehension that hawk counts alone will safeguard birds of prey, you're wasting your time down here.

"And wasting the time *I* spent here, too," he added, as he turned to regard the sun just cresting the horizon.

"But there isn't a decline," I insisted.

"There will be," he promised.

"Raptor populations are going up."

"They'll go down," he assured.

"But they haven't," I insisted.

"They haven't?" he said, quizzically. "I'd check your records if I were you. Go ahead," he encouraged. "Unless I miss my guess, it's not too early to tell. On the contrary, it might be too late."

I did check the counts, mentally, pulling the fact-checking portion of my brain off the telephone number assignment and putting him to work.

As memory served, Bald Eagle numbers were climbing steadily, recovering nicely from their brush with DDT; Osprey, too. Peregrine and Merlin numbers had shot up severalfold; harrier totals were more than double what they had been in the midseventies—of course the totals *had* been slumping since the early eighties.

"Yes, the northern and tundra breeders are all right for the present," Maurice confirmed, reading my mind. "What about some of the other species?"

Yes, he had me there. The Red-shouldered was still declining. American Kestrel numbers were just a shadow of what they had been a couple of decades ago, the shadow of a shadow. Sharp-shinneds? Yes, the trend during the eighties had been decidedly down. The recovery of the seventies was over, and the decade of decline had been too persistent to dismiss as "just a slump" or "a couple of years of bad winds." In fact, among many in the field, it was becoming evident that Sharp-shinned Hawk numbers were crashing.

I studied Maurice studying me. I knew the problem. I guess I recognized the problem even before I'd regarded the evidence.

"You're losing ground," Maurice said.

I nodded.

"And time," he added.

I nodded again.

Two harriers, too high to have gotten up with this day's sun, moved out over Delaware Bay. Their lazy, loping wing beat, visible only as a flickering cadence, was as identifiable as a fingerprint.

"What can we do to stop the decline?" I said finally.

Maurice smiled, sadly. "I don't know. It's a problem beyond my ken. The problems of the times must be dealt with by those living in those times."

"My battle," he continued, "was fought in the thirties. We fought tradition and prejudice and ignorance with lots of facts, lots of determination, and a growing public awareness, and we stopped the hawk shooting.

"In the sixties and the seventies, it was pesticides—a threat that was more insidious, harder to pinpoint, more difficult to combat; experts in white lab coats going toe to toe with other experts in white lab coats. It took researchers and data and an unstoppable public outcry to set things right. But DDT was banned in North America."

"And now the problem is habitat," I said.

"The problem is *loss* of habitat," Maurice corrected. "Loss of habitat, coupled with the incredible egocentric belief that humanity's needs are somehow different from and superior to the needs of other living things."

"And you can't suggest a solution?" I pleaded.

He didn't respond but there was a shivering flicker in his eyes—the master's momentary crossness with the student who hadn't learned his lesson. "Did you ever write your book on hawk identification?" he asked, changing the subject.

"Yes," I replied. "We did. The reviews were good. It sold forty thousand copies. We're working on a second edition now.

"We, uh, dedicated it to you," I added. "I hope you don't mind."

Maurice smiled. "No," he said, "not at all. Does it deal much with identifications from above? Dorsal views?"

"No, we're kind of weak there," I confessed.

"Too bad," he joked. "We could use a good field guide, but there isn't much call for one that emphasizes overhead silhouettes at our site."

"No, I guess that's so," I agreed. "But listen," I offered, "if you like, we can go back to the office and I can scroll up a couple of chapters I'm working on now. I've got them on disk."

"Disk?" Maurice queried, shaking his head.

"Disk. For my word processor," I explained.

"Word processor?" he pronounced, savoring each syllable as he spoke. "What is a word processor?"

"It's like a typewriter except it's easier to correct your mistakes."

"It sounds like a device admirably suited for the times," he observed wryly.

I didn't try to contradict him.

We stood for a time, thinking separate thoughts, or maybe thinking the same thought separately. It sure was odd that the two of us were the only ones on the platform. It should have been jammed by now. And where was the official hawk watcher? Where were the scores of people who travel to Cape May just to savor the flights?

"Maurice," I said finally, "are you telling me that there isn't any solution, that all raptor populations are just going to go the way of the Passenger Pigeon and for the same reason?"

"I never said that," he admonished.

"Then there is a solution and you just aren't telling?"

"I never said that, either."

I thought he wasn't going to discuss it any more, but I was wrong. "What you should do is obvious isn't it?" he coaxed. "You should protect birds of prey by protecting their habitat. The 'how' is the thing that you must determine, and that is the challenge of those whose lives are wedded to the present.

"But if you want the advice of someone who sees the present through history's window consider this: If people are the problem, people can also be the solution.

"And if I might make another suggestion," he added, "perhaps a little alacrity would be in order."

"Do we have enough time?" I asked, turning, watching the first, early Sharp-shinned Hawks getting up, hunting for breakfast in the trees north of the hawk watch.

"All the time left in the world—for better or worse," he said.

When I looked back, he was gone—leaving an empty place where he had stood that, within the hour, would be filled with hawk counters.

Koltsfoot

Below the ridge, on the south slope, spring was a certainty. The season had progressed too far to be forced into retreat by a single cold front. After all, this wasn't February.

No matter what the thermometer read, no matter what that fork-tongued, subterranean Pennsylvania rodent proclaimed, winter had shot its bolt. If you stepped below the crest, you could feel spring in the sun.

But I couldn't step over the crest of the ridge, even though that would have been the sensible thing to do—even though all along the south slope of New Jersey's Kittatinny Ridge, rabbits, raptors, red foxes, and all manner of sensible, warm-blooded creatures were doing just that.

It is the nature of humans to engage in activities that are not, strictly speaking, sensible. One of these involves standing on open ridge tops—in the path of cold northwest winds—when that is the only way there is to observe migrating hawks. And, up on top, winter was clearly in command.

The *sensible* thing to do would have been to get out of the wind. The *sensible* things to do would have been to quit this frost-blasted hilltop and head into Blairstown for a cup of coffee, or maybe go over to Floyd's and get myself invited to lunch.

These would have been the sensible things to do. Instead, I brought the binoculars up, cupped the right eyepiece with a mittened hand to keep my eye from tearing, and started another scan of the horizon.

The plateau was the color of slate in rain, not at all like the woodlands below, where maples were already blushing with spring. In deeper, shadowed ravines, there was snow; would be, in fact, into April (maybe May).

Over the Walnut Bluffs, the resident pair of Red-tailed Hawks were going through aerial gyrations. A distant smudge caught my eye, a shadow of a smudge, the barest suggestion of a flaw in the ice blue sky—a flock of migrating crows.

At two miles, a single bird would have been invisible, but a flock takes on form and this was a big flock. *Really* big for so late in the season. Two hundred in the main group, more strung out behind.

I counted, working the binoculars back along their flight path, hearing (but ignoring) the sound of someone coming up the trail. The steps were slow, labored—the sound of someone carrying a heavy pack or someone who had completed a long climb.

"Crows, Peter?" a voice inquired.

"Crows, Ed," I confirmed, making the identification by call.

So, today is Saturday. Good. Company for a slow day.

"Big flock," Ed observed from behind the barrels of his 10 × 50 Kerns (a pair of binoculars that half the hawk watchers in North America would kill to own).

"Big flock," I agreed. "Hello, Lana," I added, addressing the slight, spry figure approaching over Ed's shoulder.

"Good morning, Peter. Any hawks moving?"

"Not much. It's early yet," I added to show my optimism and to bolster hers. "The local Red-taileds are putting on a show," I added.

"Oh, well, that's nice," she said, expressing her gratitude for this shared bit of information with a quick glance toward the bluffs. "Very . . . nice," she repeated between breaths.

It's a long climb to the top of Raccoon Ridge.

I waited patiently, wanting to ask, but deciding to make a game of it instead. I wouldn't ask. I'd just wait and see.

Lana, I guess, didn't know the rules or didn't care to play.

"John's coming," she confirmed, spoiling the game.

Yes, I could see him now, coming up the trail. His eyes focused on the ground at his feet. The hatless head glistening with sweat. The walking stick favored by hikers in the old country making smooth leaps at his side. I thought of the riddle of the Sphinx.

The figure dropped from view below the rim, then reappeared in piecemeal increments: a bowed head . . . hunched shoulders . . . heavy wool coat . . . harsh, gray trousers . . . boots . . . and, finally, with a quick upward glance, a broad face supporting a mischievous grin.

"Hullow," he said through his grin.

"Hello, John," I said through one of my own.

Without another word, he walked to his favorite spot, and stood, patiently waiting for his lungs to find the wind they had lost along the way.

John was eighty. I don't know how I knew this. Someone must have told me. He was married. He lived in the city. He didn't drive. He came to the ridge on weekends when Ed and Lana invited him. His accent was German (maybe Austrian, or Czech, or Polish).

I don't know. I don't have an ear for these things.

He was a watcher, a close looker, a person who found fascination or beauty (and usually both) in whatever was at hand. He was the sort of person who might stare in silent contemplation for minutes on end, then turn, and directing your attention with his walking stick say, "This is a good rock," or "This is a good tree."

And, you know what? You would look at it . . . and it *was* a good rock. Funny, you hadn't noticed it before.

John was not a hawk watcher, per se, no more than he was a rock watcher or a tree watcher, but he looked at hawks, too, when there were any hawks to look at. And John had watched enough hawks in his time to know that this was not a particularly good day for hawk watching.

John gave us the benefit of his company for a time (to pay Ed and Lana for the ride and for their kindness). He accepted a cookie from Ed, declined coffee from Lana, visited all of his local points of interest and then announced:

"I think I will go to find *koltsfoot.*"

"Coltsfoot?" I repeated. I'd never heard of coltsfoot but

guessed that it was a flower or plant. Botany isn't my strong suit. But even I know enough about nonwoody plants to know that they didn't abide Arctic conditions and that the temperature had put ice on the reservoir the previous night.

I think John sensed my skepticism.

"Ja, koltsfoot," he affirmed. "It is very early flower." Then he ambled off, headed downridge.

I didn't think much of his odds. And I really couldn't understand why anyone would go off in search of a flower when there were hawks to be found.

That's the difference between the way a hawk watcher thinks and a close-looker thinks. The difference between twenty-five and eighty.

"Coltsfoot," Ed pronounced, after John had gone, "*Tussilago farfara.* A composite, found in damp soil, often mistaken for a dandelion. The flowers appear in March. The leaves, which resemble the foot of a colt, come later. It's a European immigrant."

Then, after a short pause he added, "Sometimes used for the treatment of coughs or asthma."

"Koltsfoot," I said, trying to put a bark in the consonants and purr in the vowels. "Koltsfoot." Neat name.

John returned in midafternoon. "There have been some hawks?" he asked.

Yes, there'd been a few; no more than you would expect for a cold day in March, but a few.

"Did you find any coltsfoot, John?" Lana inquired.

"Ja," John said, bobbing his head stiffly, emphatically, "spring is coming."

Then he smiled quickly but warmly like the sun that breaks through an overcast sky.

"Spring," he said, correcting himself, "is here. Here," he repeated, looking toward the earth at his feet and finding it.

That was many springs ago, now. And that was the last time I saw John. But last spring, while birding in the Jersey Highlands with several friends, I stopped our car to watch a pair of Red-shouldered Hawks. It was a cold windy day in March but the birds were courting ferociously.

After our eyes had taken their fill of the birds, they wandered to the roadside. There, protruding between the cast leaves of another season, were a host of small yellow flowers. Their heads tossed in the wind and they looked a bit like dandelions.

"Anybody know what kind of flowers these are?" someone inquired.

The name came unbidden and without effort.

"Coltsfoot," I said. And, after a short time, I pointed and added, "Next to that one is a good rock."

Death List

This isn't the kind of topic that you would have heard discussed at anybody's cocktail party—unless Stephen King is a birder. Its vast but macabre potential has never been bandied about at any bird club meeting or Christmas Bird Count roundup I've ever attended. And the notion of a birding "death list" probably wouldn't have surfaced at all—except we were already *that* close to death. A hundred miles off the coast of New Jersey. Clinging to ice-encrusted rails in heavy seas. Praying for the vision of a Great Skua or the mercy of a bullet in the temple (and not necessarily in that order).

"I think I'm going to be sick," said Jim.

"I think I'm going to be sick and die," said Vince.

"I think I'm going to be sick and die before I can put skua on my life list," said Clay, pushing the needle on the loss register all the way to the right.

"I think if you're dead," said Vince (who even dying is a most philosophical fellow), "that you won't be able to put it on your life list, Clay."

"Then I'll put it on my . . . *ulp* . . . death list," said Clay. "You guys can just toss me overboard and the bird can have my remains."

"Hey," I said, intrigued by Clay's heroic offer. "Maybe you've got something there."

I don't know about you, but I've always been ambivalent about the prospects of burial *and* cremation. Small, dark places give me the willies, but I also don't like to think that the es-

A Field
Guide
BIRDS
of
Keith Hansen 1993

sence of my being could fit in a vase and lie dormant on the top shelf of my closet.

But now, thanks to Clay's visionary leap, there's an alternative that's recycling-sensitive, environmentally sound—and it will make serious listers who died before this new category was implemented just spin in their graves. Consider the merits of using your earthly remains to attract birds. I say if a body is good enough to push up daisies, it's good enough to pull down a few good birds.

I'll bet you think the possibilities are limited, right? A couple of vultures, crows, ravens, magpies—maybe an eagle or two. Certainly nothing to *die* for.

Ah, but just set your mind to it and let your imagination run. Consider, for instance, how many birds you could attract just by handing out a few locks of hair. Consider Northern Orioles!

Everybody who read the same out-of-date books I did when I was growing up knows that orioles suspend their nests from strands of horse hair. But ever since the internal combustion engine was slapped on a chassis, orioles have had to struggle to find enough hair. For all anybody knows, oriole populations might have crashed as a result of Henry Ford's invention.

Well, if the idea of a death list catches on, we could have orioles nesting from every limb—and you, Mr. or Ms. Parts Donor, would be an integral part of the recovery program. Wouldn't that be better than having your dust gathering dust in a plastic-lined box in the closet while friends and relatives debate whether to spread your ashes at Hawk Mountain or Cave Creek Canyon?

Consider bones! Ospreys will carry anything to their nest. Imagine one of your very own ribs feathering an osprey nest, tucked right in there with the fishing line and broken beach chairs. Imagine having a Lammergeier putting a shin bone of yours into free fall.

And wouldn't you just *die* to have a bubbly little House Wren singing from the occipital orbit of your very own philanthropic noggin?

Every species of bird you attract to your remains counts as one on your death list.

Few places exist where the ranges of House Wrens and Lammergeiers overlap—none in fact. Like generating a big life list, mustering a big death list demands mobility. Since death is somewhat immobilizing, serious death listers will need help spreading their wealth around. No doubt there will have to be different categories for single-assist and multiple-assist death lists.

A Death List Rules Committee will also have to address things like secondary (fatal) attractants. Can a body, for instance, claim a Say's Phoebe that is attracted to the insect hatch associated with strategically placed viscera (but not the viscera themselves)? Does a Golden Bowerbird count if it stashes one of your gold-filled molars in its bower (but ignores cavity-free teeth)?

And getting back to skuas, if some vital organ is merely added to the chum, does any skua that plops down in the slick count, or does a body only get credited with an assist?

These questions and others remain. But the potential of this new category is so limitless it fairly takes your breath away. After all, a life list only lasts a lifetime. But a death list! Well, a death list lasts as long as you do.